I0558957

Back to the garden

The magic of gardening therapy

Anne Dubitzky

**blind cat
press**

Back to the garden
The magic of gardening therapy

Photography	Anne Dubitzky
Book design	Margherita Buzzi
Typeface	Iowan Old Style

ISBN Paperback: 979-8-9898985-0-3
ISBN Hardback: 979-8-9898985-1-0

Table of contents

*"The LORD God planted a garden in Eden, in the east,
and placed there the man whom He had formed."*
Genesis 2:8

Introduction

According to the Biblical creation story, plants were created on the third day and man on the sixth (Genesis 1:11-13, 26). In the second chapter of Genesis, God placed man in the Garden of Eden, to till it and tend it. (Genesis 2:8, 15) Whether one believes in the Bible as the revealed word of God or views Genesis as an archetypal myth of the origins of the world, the centrality of the garden in the story of humanity is indisputable. Man and woman began in the garden, became custodians of the garden and were eventually exiled from the garden.

Ever since, people have expressed their longing to return to that primeval state of innocence, the paradise of the garden, in liturgy and folk tales. The Greek word *paradeisos* (an enclosed royal park) has its origin in the ancient Persian *pairdaeza*, which similarly signifies an enclosure or park. The word for heaven or paradise in Hebrew is *gan eden* ("garden of Eden"), and another Hebrew word for paradise is *pardes* ("orchard"). Across a variety of cultures, the concept of heaven is associated with a garden.

Whether or not heaven is a garden, research has shown that exposure to plants has a measurably positive impact on mood[1]. Even being in a room with photos of plants can have a salutary effect on a person's mental state. The effect increases as one moves from photos to a view of greenery through a window to physically being in a garden or out in nature. And the therapeutic value of working directly with plants and soil can be dramatic. I would posit that these findings are the result of something built into our DNA—the drive to get back to "the garden," to a state of nature, to a simpler time, to connect with Mother Earth and the plants that spring from her.

After retiring from a career as a lawyer and a healthcare administrator, first in Boston and later in Israel, I enrolled in a program at Seminar HaKibbutzim, a local college in Tel Aviv, to become a gardening therapist. The curriculum includes courses in psychology, anthropology and horticulture, with a smattering of arts and crafts. As

---

1   One of the seminal works on this subject is Kaplan R., Kaplan S. (1989). *The Experience of Nature: A Psychological Perspective.* Cambridge: Cambridge University Press

part of our horticultural training, students were given small garden plots to cultivate and tend.

Gardening or horticultural, therapy, began as a discipline in England after World War II. As veterans returned from the front suffering from "shell shock" (now called PTSD), someone had the idea that since the English were known to be avid gardeners, perhaps gardening could reach these men and help them reintegrate into society. It worked, and the field proliferated. Gardening therapy programs were brought to hospitals, old-age homes, schools, and even prisons. The practice gained traction in the US, Europe, Israel, and elsewhere around the world.

My training included an internship at Reut Rehabilitation Hospital, where I have worked as a volunteer ever since. The hospital treats a wide range of patients: short-term inpatients who are there for a few weeks or months for intensive physical and occupational therapy following surgery or an injury; long-term residents on "complex medical" floors, who tend to be people who have had strokes or brain injuries, some cognitively intact, others with more limited cognitive function; patients on ventilators, some with ALS and other kinds of paralysis, who are bedridden; and ambulatory day patients, who may have been inpatients at one time but now come a couple of days a week for a period of months, to receive various therapies. The patients range in age from children (though the gardening therapy program does not include children) to the very elderly.

The hospital has had a therapeutic garden on its roof for about 20 years. The plants in the garden are all in pots or flower boxes. Except for the trees, which grow in large pots set directly on the floor, most of the plants are arranged on raised tables, shelves, and beds (which are actual old hospital beds, recycled as platforms for potted plants). In this way, the plants in the garden are accessible to patients in wheelchairs and those who are unable to stoop or bend.

The stories in this book are drawn from my

experiences at Reut. The names of patients and identifying details have been changed to protect their privacy, in accordance with Israeli confidentiality requirements. Many of the events I describe occurred during the COVID era. Thus, in addition to being an account of my work as a gardening therapist, it is also a chronicle of how the pandemic affected the functioning of the hospital, impacted my patients, and influenced me as a caregiver.

Over the years, I have been privileged to meet dozens of patients who struggle with monumental physical, cognitive, and psychological challenges. I am in awe of their strength and perseverance. The families of patients, who visit them daily, and work tirelessly to help even the most severely incapacitated patients maintain a sense of dignity, have inspired and moved me. And, I have the deepest respect for the staff of the institution who, day in and day out, treat every patient with compassion, sensitivity, and professionalism.

I have illustrated the patient stories with my photographs. Although I have been an amateur photographer all my life, photography has become a more serious pursuit since I moved to Israel. I work in many genres, but in recent years, still-life photography, especially of flowers, fruit, and vegetables has been a particular passion of mine. I am drawn to the miraculous complexity and perfection of flowers and their ephemeral beauty, which I try to capture and preserve in photos.

As I wrote the text and shot the photographs for this book, it occurred to me that the satisfaction I feel working with patients with disabilities and the pleasure I find in photography derive from the same source. As a photographer, I am inclined (some may say driven) to find and photograph what is beautiful, particularly the surprising, unexpected glimmers of beauty in what may otherwise seem ugly or, at best, ordinary. I look at vacant lots in Tel Aviv and see the wildflowers in bloom. My photos look like they might have been taken in an open field of anemones and buttercups, far from the city with no sign of the discarded bottles and cast-off furniture or the derelict building next door. One of my favorite subjects is wilting flowers. I look for the beauty in imperfection—what the Japanese call *wabi sabi*.

Photography is about focus and framing—what you choose to focus on, and how you frame it or isolate it from its surroundings. From my experience, the same is true working with profoundly compromised patients. When I talk to friends about my severely incapacitated patients, they often ask, "Isn't it depressing?" "No," I reply. I seek patients' strengths and focus on those. But it's also a matter of framing. When I am with a patient in the ventilator unit, it can be overwhelming to try to take in the larger picture— the monitors, the tubes, the vegetative patient in the next bed. For the moment, I ignore the context—that this poor woman is alive thanks to a tube in her throat attached to a pump in the wall and cannot move from her bed. Instead, I look at the sparkle in her eyes when I show her a flower and the smile on her lips when she inhales the scent of a sprig of lavender. And just as the challenge for me when I photograph a flower is somehow to capture and preserve its ephemeral beauty, likewise with my patients. I try to hold on to the signs of pleasure or at least a reaction and expand on them. Once I find something that elicits a positive response, I use that stimulus—a flower, a fragrant herb, a textured leaf—to encourage the patient to do more. I try to help them reach their full potential, however limited that might be.

And for those patients whose condition will not improve or who are declining, I focus on what skills and senses remain, hoping to enable them to enjoy the beauty, scent, or simply the texture of a flower or a plant. When a patient blinks their eyes in response to a fragrant herb or the "fur" of a sage leaf on his cheek, it is a beautiful moment, and I share in his pleasure and leave the room smiling. Plants have worked their magic on both of us.

I hope that through these stories my readers, too, will come to appreciate the magic and power of plants.

13

Chapter 1

Like a Woman in the Delivery Room

I met Mina during my internship. Every time I went to the hospital, I saw her seated in her wheelchair in front of one of the computers in a room adjacent to the roof garden. Her straight, mousy brown hair, starting to gray, was held back with a headband or gathered into a ponytail. She had a pleasant face, with smooth, unlined skin and pale, gray-blue eyes. She appeared to be in her late thirties or early forties. Mina had overheard me speaking in English on occasion and was eager to practice her English with me. We would sometimes chat as I arrived or left the garden.

Mina stood out from the other patients I'd seen at the hospital. She was not in rehab from surgery or an injury, nor did she require full-time care. She smoothly navigated the corridors of the institution in her wheelchair, which she maneuvered with one hand. I soon realized that she was a long-term resident who did not fit into any framework offered by the institution. It seemed a shame that she spent her days playing on the computer while listening to 1990s songs.

When I returned after completing my internship, I asked one of the therapists whether I might be able to do individual therapy with Mina if she were interested. I thought that working in the garden would add interest and variety to Mina's life. I also hoped that seeing plants she had planted grow, flower, and bear fruit might help her feel productive. The garden would be a place where she could be creative, make decisions, and exercise responsibility. My colleague replied that Mina was sometimes prickly, with a tough shell that was not very permeable. My reaction was: "I'm a grown-up, I think I can handle this. Let's give it a try." When I asked Mina if she would be interested in working with me in the garden for half an hour a week, she replied enthusiastically. She told me she loved the garden and plants. We fixed a time for our weekly meetings and embarked on our journey.

Mina had an old-style flip phone that hung on a lanyard around her neck, and she would use it to call her sister and tell her each time she went with me into the garden. Likewise, at the end of each session, she would call her sister to report that she was going back inside. During our first meeting, I gave Mina a tour of the garden. She was wide mouthed with awe as I pointed out the various vegetables growing from vines, the colorful profusion of pansies, roses, and snapdragons. She was amazed to see fluffy wads of cotton growing on plants. The herb and succulent corners thrilled her.

Before beginning any project in the garden with Mina, I slipped a gardening apron over her head and spread the skirt of the apron to cover her right arm, which rested motionless on the tray of her wheelchair. Not only is Mina paralyzed from the waist down, but she has the use of only one hand. During our time working together, I was repeatedly struck by how much she could do with that one hand.

Mina enjoyed digging in the soil and had no problem dirtying her left hand, with its long, slim fingers and neatly manicured but unpolished, nails. However, it was very important to her that her useless right hand be kept clean. Mina was always well-groomed and neatly dressed. She was adamant that her clothes not be soiled, and most of all, it was essential that the gleaming white sports shoes on her feet remain immaculate. Although she never discussed this, at some point it occurred to me that Mina was not able to dress or undress herself. In fact, on rare occasions, she arrived late for her session, explaining that the orderlies came to get her out of bed later than usual. If her clothes needed to be changed, she had to ask an aide to undress and re-dress her. It would be difficult to find a busy staff member to do that. Having dirty clothes thus reinforced Mina's sense of dependence. By insisting that I protect the cleanliness of her clothes and shoes, she was able to exercise a small modicum of control over her environment.

The only time Mina lost her composure with me was when I spilled some potting soil and a few bits of dirt landed on her white shoes. She flew into a rage. I apologized profusely and wiped the dirt off her shoes, and we continued our project. On reflection, I understood Mina's distress about the dirt. I had damaged her "perfect" look and disrupted her controlled appearance. It was almost as if I had exposed her "inner dirt," namely her wounds and dependency. The following week, I asked about the incident of the dirt on her shoes. She laughed and said it was nothing, that she'd already forgotten about it. This was certainly not the Mina that my colleagues had talked about—prone to anger and negative emotions, often demanding and unforgiving. In the three years we worked together in the garden, only twice did I witness examples of those tendencies.

I asked Mina if there was something in particular she would like to do for our first project in the garden. She told me that she wanted to grow vegetables. We decided that we would start with cherry tomatoes. They germinate quickly and bear fruit quickly. In addition, the plants continue to produce for many months. I brought several cherry tomatoes from home. We decided to do an experiment. Usually, one would remove the seeds from the fruit (or tomato), dry them, and then germinate them in soil (or on damp towels). Instead, our plan was to leave the seeds inside the tomatoes and see whether they would sprout. Mina understood that this was an experiment, that there was a chance that it would fail, and that seeds might not sprout this way. Nonetheless, she was eager to give it a try.

I held each tomato as Mina deftly cut it in half with a paring knife. Using a spade, she filled a couple of dozen small seedling pots with potting soil. She planted half a tomato in each small pot. Then, she watered all the plants with a watering can. Finally, with great pride, as I held the plastic stake down, she wrote her name, the date, and "cherry tomato" with a waterproof marker on the signs we inserted into each tray of pots. It was very important to Mina not only that her plants be labeled but that she be the one who wrote the labels. When were finished, she wheeled herself to the small greenhouse on the roof and I placed the trays of pots inside.

In Israel, tomatoes have two growing seasons. They can be planted from February through early March, and again from mid-August through mid-September. As a result, one can have ripe cherries tomatoes in the garden almost all year round.

The following week, Mina arrived at the roof garden a half hour early for our session (this happened often—as she was eager to have as much time as possible in the garden). I greeted her, asking how she was. She said that she was "wonderful" and told me that any time she spends in the garden she is happy. She only wishes we could meet every day. (For safety reasons, patients are only allowed in the garden with a therapist, so she was only

17

able to enter the garden during our sessions.) After a brief tour of the garden to see what had bloomed or borne fruit since the previous week, Mina was eager to see whether there had been any progress in our tomato experiment. I went to the greenhouse and brought out the trays of pots marked with Mina's name.

Sure enough, every single pot contained several tiny green sprouts, each with a pair of miniature bright green leaves!! Mina was thrilled. "I feel like a woman in the delivery room!" she exclaimed. Tears welled in my eyes. Here was a woman in her early forties who had never had a child and never would, to whom the thrill of seeing her tomato seeds sprout felt comparable to the joy of giving birth.

Two weeks later, the tomato plants had grown enough that it was time to transfer them to larger pots. Unlike some patients, who are loath to discard any seedlings, Mina had no prob-

18

lem thinning the sprouts. She then gently removed each remaining seedling with its ball of dirt from the tiny pot, filled larger pots with soil, repotted the tomato plants, and watered them all. I cleared several shelves along one wall of the garden, which we designated as "Mina's Garden." It was soon full of brightly colored seasonal flowers and a variety of vegetables she had planted.

After a couple more weeks, the tomato plants had grown tall enough that they needed to be staked. Mina put stakes in the pots, and I helped her fasten the stems to the stakes. She noticed small yellow blossoms on the tomato plants and was fasci-

nated to learn that a plant needs to flower before it can bear fruit, and that the same was true of vegetables such as peppers, beans, and peas. "I never knew that a plant had to flower before it could bear fruit," she said with awe and surprise. We talked about how the flowers are pollinated, enabling seeds to form. I explained that the fruit, or tomato or pepper, carries the seeds of the plant.

As the weeks passed, the yellow flowers turned into tiny green fruit, and the green tomatoes grew and ripened into bright red cherry tomatoes. Mina and I adopted the custom of beginning each week's session by picking ripe, sun-warmed tomatoes off the vines in Mina's Garden and enjoying a little snack together before tackling the project at hand. Mina's joy and enthusiasm for the produce she had grown was infectious. She could not tell me often enough how happy she was in the garden and how much she loved planting seeds or cuttings and watching them grow.

Occasionally, she would notice small holes in the leaves of her tomato or pepper plants. She was angry that an insect or a snail had been nibbling in her garden. She wondered how they got there. I explained that there may be insects in the soil, but that many of them fly or crawl all over the roof garden in search of tasty plants and fruit. Since we don't use pesticides in the garden, we must learn to live with the pests. Mina never found that response satisfying. Her reaction suggested to me that she had difficulty accepting that adversity is ubiquitous and that bad things can happen. She may also have been uncomfortable with the fact that the hospital didn't make efforts to protect the plants from creatures that might try to harm them.

Mina and I also planted potatoes. I brought her a few old potatoes with eyes that I found in the root bin at home. While I held the potato, Mina cut it into sections, each with at least one eye. She then filled a large empty potting soil bag, which I put into a large flowerpot, with a mixture of soil and compost, and planted the potato sections in the soil, making sure they were well covered with potting mix. Mina watered the soil, and we set the pot in a shady area of the garden. Each week, I would bring the big pot to Mina so she could check whether there had been any growth. After a few weeks, we were both delighted to see green sprouts poking out of the soil in the bag. I instructed Mina to add soil to the pot to cover the new growth. The concept here is that one continues to add soil to cover the new stems and leaves so that the plant puts its energy into growing the tubers (potatoes) in the soil, rather than growing stems and leaves. Once the soil level reaches the top of the bag, we can allow the leaves to grow until they eventually wilt. That signals that the potatoes are ready to be harvested.

Every week, Mina and I eagerly looked at the progress of the potato plants and covered the new growth with soil, until one day, we looked in the pot and there was nothing there. No trace of the previous weeks' growth remained. We were staring into a bag of dirt! I picked up the pot to let Mina reach her hand into the soil at the bottom of the bag—nothing. Either insects or, more likely, a fungus or disease had attacked our previously thriving potato plants and killed them. I felt awful. I was concerned about how disappointed Mina might feel. On reflection, I think I was more upset than she was. She did not evince any of the anger she had displayed when she saw that insects or snails had been eating her pepper plants. We talked again about how there are no guarantees of success in gardening. "That's okay," she said, "that happens." I was struck by the difference in her response to failure of the potatoes from her reaction to the holes in the leaves of the tomato and pepper plants. Either she had learned to flow more with the ups and downs of gardening, or, possibly, she did not feel as invested in the invisible potatoes as she did in the vegetables whose growth she had watched from week to week.

Although I addressed such issues with patients like Mina, I generally avoided confronting failure with my sicker patients—those in the complex medical unit or the ventilator unit. My feeling was that these people are dealing with enough hardship, and it's better to keep gardening a positive experience for them. Consequently, when patients on the complex medical floor planted several trays of seeds, I only brought them those trays whose seeds had sprouted and not ones in which nothing came up. I still wonder if this is the right approach. While I want my patients to take pride and find pleasure in their accomplishments, perhaps it is not my role to shield them from failure, which is an unavoidable aspect of gardening —and life. My decision not to face disappointment with these patients may reflect my own discomfort at dealing with issues of loss more than it does sound therapeutic thinking. After all, in light of their life circumstances, many of these individuals already have the resilience to absorb disappointing messages.

Mina delighted in every aspect of the garden. She enjoyed weeding and pruning not only her own plants but other plants and bushes in the garden. From her wheelchair, she was able to reach the lower branches and cut off dead leaves. In the late spring and early summer, when the pitangos (Surinam cherries) ripened, Mina would direct me to the brightest red fruits hanging on the trees in the corner of the garden and ask me to pick them for her so she could eat them. She never complained about the weather in the garden. In the winter, she relished the feeling of the wind in her hair, and in the summer, she basked in the warmth of the sun on her shoulders.

Mina has been confined to medical institutions most of her life from the age of 14. At the rehab hospital, her "home" was a bed in a room 4 meters by 4 meters, which she shared with two elderly, bedridden, women who had dementia. It was no wonder she was eager to spend her time upstairs on the computer—or better yet, outside in the garden.

Over time, I learned from members of the staff that Mina's story is a particularly tragic one. Mina and her family emigrated from Eastern Europe to Israel when Mina was a young child, and her father died shortly thereafter. When she was 14 years old, her mother was shot and killed by a terrorist. Mina was also shot in the melee when she tried to protect her mother by inserting herself between her and the shooter. Her injuries were severe: She was paralyzed from the waist down and lost the use of her right hand. Her vision in one eye is impaired, and she suffers from cognitive deficits.

Mina was not the only patient I encountered whose incapacity was the result of a terrorist attack. Ari, a 40-year-old man, confined to his wheelchair, with two useless legs, one useless arm and dramatic scars on his head, was another example. Every day, he wheeled himself with his one good hand up to the computers adjacent to the garden. He laughed when I offered to work with him in the garden. He had his own agenda on the internet. Ari had been injured in a terrorist bombing when he was a teenager and had resided in the hospital ever since. His story and Mina's cause me to think about the countless Israelis, particularly young people, who have been injured, many of them gravely, in terrorist incidents over the years. The newspapers always announce the number killed and injured in an attack. They also generally recite the name, age, and other details of those who died, sometimes printing photos of their funerals and excerpts of the eulogies. But the injured remain only a number. No one talks about those whose lives are permanently, often devastatingly, altered by the injuries they sustained. Seeing Mina and Ari reminded me of the enormous toll the intifadas and subsequent terrorist attacks have taken on Israeli society, and the huge social cost.

Not once during the years I worked with her, did Mina ever mention to me the circumstances of her injury, nor did she ever refer to her physical limitations. In addition to talking about the plants, flowers, and projects in the garden, Mina spoke to me about the movies (mostly American movies) she watched on the internet. A favorite movie of hers was Ghost, starring Whoopie Goldberg and Patrick Swayze. (I really must see this movie one of these days.) Most of the time we worked together, Mina and I spoke in Hebrew. She would occasionally correct my Hebrew or teach me words I didn't know. But when it came to plants, she referred to me as "the teacher" and deferred to my "expertise."

During the COVID crisis, Mina abruptly left the rehab hospital, where she had lived for almost 20 years, to move in with her sister. As I reflected on Mina's situation, I realized that she has much in common with the original gardening therapy patients, the shell-shocked British World War II vets; in addition to her severe physical limitations, she suffers from PTSD. Her work with me in the garden was precisely what she needed to help her feel she could control and have a positive impact on her environment. In the garden, she was no longer a victim, a passive patient dependent on hospital staff to get her out of bed, dress her, bring her food. She could choose to plant seeds, nurture them, and help them grow into plants whose fruit she could eat and share. It is hardly surprising that Mina, whose selfless act rendered her almost helpless, should at times be angry or resentful. It is, however, wondrous that gardening could bring joy and peace to her soul.

Chapter 2

A Daisy Blooms in the Ventilator Unit

I will never forget my first visit to the ventilator unit. A disturbing, indescribable odor—at once medicinal and putrid—assault-
ed me. It permeated the unit. After a few minutes, I no longer
noticed it, yet every time I entered, that odor struck me anew.
The unit was a maze of large rooms without doors, each with
several beds, each containing a motionless person with a large
tube connecting their throat to a pump on the wall. Some wore
plastic oxygen masks on their faces. Others had faces contorted
into ghoulish masks. There were those with curled limbs, hands
gnarled into claws, or legs gathered into a fetal position. Many
looked like mummies, stretched out neatly on their backs with
a placid look on their faces and seemingly unseeing eyes facing
the ceiling. Each bed was surrounded by monitors emitting beeps
and occasional more urgent-sounding alarms, while electronic
screens cast an otherworldly greenish glow on everything in the
room. There was almost no natural light in the unit. Most of the
few windows had their shades drawn.

Entering this environment, I was viscerally conflict-
ed between my urge to stare and my desire not to see. I felt
simultaneously a morbid fascination and a responsibility to afford
these poor souls some measure of privacy and respect. This could
happen to me or, God forbid, to someone I loved. In an instant,
a stroke or an accident had transformed each of these patients
from a walking, talking, working, loving person into a carapace.
Yet, in many cases, a wife, a husband, a son, or a daughter sat at
the bedside of these seeming shells of human beings, stroking
their hands, talking lovingly to them, or playing music, perhaps
knowing or perhaps only hoping that their loved one could at
least hear and feel their presence and know that they were still
loved and not forgotten.

One might reasonably ask what role a gardening therapist can play in such a unit. How can we possibly help these
patients? I was told beforehand that plants in soil are not allowed
on the unit, as particles of soil can get into the air and thus into
the lungs of these very vulnerable patients. However, cut flowers,
plant cuttings, herbs, seeds, seed pods, and other vegetable matter
were permissible. Still, what do we DO with these people? How
can we interact with them?

When I started visiting patients on the ventilator
unit, I felt overwhelmed by the tragedy of their circumstances
—people who can't speak, who communicate only by moving their
eyes, people who are blind and paralyzed, people who can't even
breathe without mechanical assistance. But with time, I started to
see these people differently. As I got to know individual patients,
my focus shifted from their disabilities to their abilities. And, I
discovered, even on the ventilator unit, patients' conditions vary
greatly. The sweet spot of gardening therapy in such a setting is
finding activities that speak to what each patient can do.

One patient had been a professor of biochemistry. Now
confined to a bed, on a ventilator, she expressed great interest
in the flowers and plants I brought to her. Another patient, with
ALS, raised her eyebrows when I showed her yellow flowers.

When I left her a small bouquet of red and pink flowers in a cup, she showed her pleasure with her eyes. A suggestion of a smile appeared on her lips when I gave her flowers to smell. In contrast to other units, where gardening serves both occupational therapy and psychotherapeutic goals, in the ventilator unit it is primarily intended to provide sensory stimulation, a bit of variety in an otherwise endlessly monotonous routine.

Offering patients herbs to smell and identify very often led to a conversation about the foods one associates with a particular herb. You can hardly smell fresh mint without thinking and talking about mint tea or *limonana* (a popular local lemonade with crushed mint) or tabouli or fattoush salad. The powerful fragrance of basil evokes thoughts (and discussion) of pasta, pesto, and other Italian dishes. But after chatting with patients about these associations, it occurred to me that perhaps it is unfair or inappropriate to be rhapsodizing about foods and flavors with patients whose diet consists of a bland liquid fed directly to their stomachs through a tube. I discussed this with some of the more experienced therapists, who felt that it was not a problem and that this was a way to arouse good memories and keep these people in touch with a more "normal" life. Perhaps.

The ventilator unit was the first unit I worked on when I began as a gardening-therapy intern. And, as shocking and disturbing as it was initially, it was probably the best place to cut my teeth as a therapist. Working with the patients in this unit taught me to scale down my expectations, a lesson that continues to serve me well with patients in all settings. In addition to their obvious physical limitations, most of the patients on this unit suffer from a variety of complex medical conditions. While they may superficially appear the same from day to day and week to week, like everyone, these individuals have better and worse days. One of the patients, an older woman named Hannah, enthusiastically took the vine leaves I had brought to show her and showed me how to fold them to make stuffed grape leaves. Yet the following week, she told me that she didn't feel well enough for a visit.

On one occasion, I handed a red geranium to a patient named Aziza. She asked for more. I gave her more flowers, and together we trimmed the stems to put them in a cup of water to sit as a tiny bouquet next to her bed. Her bed happened to be adjacent to one of the few windows in the unit, and she made sure that the shades were kept up. Someone had planted flowers in a window box outside her window. They looked bedraggled and sparse. Aziza asked me if I would plant more flowers in her window box. "With pleasure," I replied. I took her flowerbox with me back up to the garden and restocked it with a riot of brightly colored flowers. The next time I was on the unit, I installed Aziza's refreshed planter on the sill outside her window. She was delighted. Unfortunately, on subsequent visits, Aziza was much weaker. I made bouquets for her, as she didn't have the strength to help cut the stems. She could just manage a smile in response.

I once showed a patient named Margo a flower whose Hebrew name is the same as the word for a lazy person. She replied, "Like me." I laughed. It's hard to think of someone who is bedridden and mostly paralyzed as lazy. But it warmed my heart to see that she retained her sense of humor. I asked her how many children she has. She showed me four fingers. Margo was short for Margarit, which is one of the Hebrew words for daisy (like the French word, *marguerite*). I'd tease her and tell her that she was a flower. She was tickled when I brought her a *margarit* hold and trim. Another day, I handed her a rose to smell. She inhaled deeply and smiled a smile of recognition. I showed her colorful snapdragons I had cut in the garden. In Israel, they are considered winter flowers, but in the shade, they sometimes continue to bloom throughout the summer as well. One sees plots of jolly snapdragons, planted to add a festive touch to urban traffic circles and public parks.

Snapdragons are a favorite of mine to bring to bedridden patients—not only for their cheerful hues but because they are fun. The Hebrew name for snapdragon is *low ari* ("lion's jaw"). In Arabic, I learned, it is called the "fish flower" because it resembles

the mouth of a fish. And, indeed, if you pinch the flower laterally, its upper and lower halves open and snap shut like the jaws of a lion or the mouth of a dragon or fish. I can hold the flower and, like a puppeteer, make it "talk" to the patient.

Margo didn't feel like talking, but she indicated that she was OK with my talking about flowers. The following week, when I showed Margo flowers and gave her herbs to smell, she was not very responsive. A week later, when I approached her bedside, I saw that her eyes were closed. I gently cajoled her into opening them to look at a flower. I also gave her a sprig of mint to smell. Clearly, she was feeling weak. But on my next visit, she opened her eyes wide as soon as I arrived. She reached out to hold the flower I offered her. She smiled and wanted to keep the flower. On a subsequent visit, Margo again appeared enervated, so I simply read her a story.

One learns to take cues from the patient and let them set the pace of the session. Many times, I prepared material for patients only to find that they were sleeping or in too much pain to participate in even the simplest activity. I couldn't let myself be disappointed. I was here for them and not the other way around. And, particularly with the ventilator unit patients, I needed to remind myself that even when they didn't have the energy for any activity, merely stopping by their bed, smiling, greeting them by name, and asking how they were doing afforded them some relief from the tedium of life in a place whose unrelenting soundtrack is the beep of a monitor and the whoosh of a ventilator.

One of the most memorable patients in the ventilator unit was Michal. A woman in her 60s, she had the look of a plump child. Michal suffered from underlying developmental deficits, was blind, and had no sense of smell. Notwithstanding her many challenges, she was always in a cheerful mood. Michal was blessed with two devoted older sisters who took turns visiting her daily. They spent hours traveling by bus (or several buses) from the small city where they had lived all their lives to see their "little sister," only to be asked to leave at the end of the visiting hour.

Michal's sisters looked so much alike that, initially, I didn't realize that it wasn't always the same sister visiting her.

Michal and her sisters had animated conversations. Even if I couldn't overhear what they were saying, their laughter was electric. Whenever I brought Michal flowers, herbs, or fruit to touch, her sisters would remind her of the fruit trees and other plants that grew in the large garden of their childhood home. In the somber twilight zone of the ventilator unit, Michal was a small ray of sunshine.

Michal and her sisters called to mind the Native American legend of the three "sisters."—squash, corn (maize), and beans, three crops planted together in mounds that provide mutual support and benefit. The corn grows tall, serving as a trellis for the climbing bean stalks. The beans fix nitrogen in the soil for the corn, while their twining vines help support the corn stalks in the wind. The broad leaves of the squash cover the ground at the base of the corn and beans to shade the soil and

help it retain moisture; and the bristly hairs on the squash plants deter pests such as deer and raccoons who might have designs on any of the sisters. Native Americans have been planting the three sisters in this manner for thousands of years, and stories of these three crops, which were key to subsistence, figure prominently in the lore and customs of many Native American cultures. While I am not aware that the three-sister method of planting has taken root in Israel, the relationship of these crops evokes that of Michal and her sisters, and they found the story amusing.

Because Michal couldn't see, we appealed to her sense of touch. I brought her fuzzy leaves, prickly pinecones, fluffy wads of cotton, and smooth succulents to feel. I would ask her to guess what she was touching. Sometimes I stroked her cheek with a soft sage leaf. Michal had only partial use of her hands, but she enjoyed removing the dead leaves from the stems of flowers. On occasion, we did "experiments," like soaking a pinecone in water to see (or feel) it close. We also tried it in reverse, starting with a smooth, closed pinecone and letting it dry until it was open and spiky.

Sometimes, I would give Michal a cutting of an herb. She would pick off the lower leaves and put the stem in a cup of water. I would then leave the cup on the stand next to her bed and wait for the roots to grow. Once the cutting had sprouted roots, Michal would take delight in feeling the delicate roots emerging from the bottom of the stem. I told her I would plant the cutting in soil and put it in the greenhouse for her and report back regularly on its progress.

For variety, I sometimes read Michal stories about flowers, plants, or a magical garden. One day, we had a conversation about witches, potions, and concoctions made from herbs. A favorite story of Michal's, which I read in Hebrew to several of the patients in the ventilator unit, is the classic Chinese parable of the empty pot[2].

In the story, the childless Chinese emperor seeks to find a suitable boy to be his heir. He decides to hold a contest. The emperor invites boys from across the land to come to the palace.

33

2   Guillain, Charlotte; *The Empty Pot, A Chinese Folk Tale*; Heinemann Library 2015

Each boy is given a single seed to plant. The boy whose plant grows the largest would become heir to the emperor's throne.

One of the boys, a poor boy named Cheng, was a good gardener and very hard-working. He carefully took his seed home, planted it in a pot, and watered it daily. The other boys in his village did the same. But, as time passed, there was no sign of Cheng's seed growing, while the other boys' seeds had grown into tall plants, full of leaves. The boys boasted about how well their seeds were growing. Still, Cheng's seed did not grow. Cheng put his seed in a bigger pot, but nothing happened.

After six months, the emperor called all the boys back to the palace. The other boys arrived carrying pots with huge leafy plants, flowers, and fruits. Cheng only had an empty pot. When the emperor saw Cheng's empty pot, he smiled. He told the boys, "The seeds I gave you had been cooked. None of them could grow. Cheng was the only honest boy among you. He shall be the next emperor." So, Cheng and his family moved into the palace, and when Cheng grew up, he became one of the greatest emperors China had ever known.

Michal loved this story, as did the other patients I read it to. The story not only teaches an important life lesson about honesty, but it has a special message for gardeners. We can learn and benefit even from empty pots and the seeds that fail to sprout.

Michal responded with excitement each time I approached her bed and said her name. I marvel at how something as simple as feeling a furry leaf or a plump succulent afforded her such welcome stimulation and elicited smiles and laughter. Michal sets a powerful example. She can neither see nor smell, is fed through a tube, and lives in a bed but is nonetheless able to experience and spread joy.

Chapter 3

A Beloved Child

Ahuva also lives in the ventilator unit. As I approach her room, I
see her seated in her wheelchair, tethered to an air pump in the
wall via a large plastic tube attached to a short pipe protruding
from her throat. Her full moon face shines above her round,
bloated body. She projects a gentle innocence. Above her high
forehead, her thin hair, dyed light brown but with a bit of gray at
the roots, is pulled back and gathered in a colorful hair tie. In a
unit where most patients lie inert on their beds in hospital pajamas, Ahuva is always dressed in tasteful long-sleeved knit shirts
and matching knit pants. Delicate "gemmed" earrings hang from
her ears, and brightly colored beaded bracelets, the kind a child
might make, are wrapped around her thin wrists, drawing attention to her swollen hands and fingers. A pulse oximeter is clipped
to the index finger of her left hand. When I arrive, I usually find
her gazing up at the TV hanging from the ceiling above her bed,
watching a children's cartoon show. The cheerful high-pitched
voices of the characters clash with the grim surroundings.

The two other beds in Ahuva's room are occupied by men, both seemingly in vegetative states. One lies flat on his back, eyes open, staring blankly at the ceiling. I have never seen a visitor with him, only the occasional orderly coming to shave his face with an electric razor. The other bed contains a man whose face is grossly disfigured with what appear to be burn scars. His hands, missing several fingers, are curled, clutching tiny pillows. Most of the time, a white cloth covers his eyes. His wife visits him almost every day. She brushes his teeth and talks to him quietly as she gently rubs lotion into his skin. I've never seen him move. This man, I learned, was injured as a young soldier in the Six-Day War in 1967. His wife has been visiting him nearly daily for over 50 years!

"Good morning, Ahuva," I greet her. She turns away from the television, looks at me, and mouths "Good morning." The tube in her throat prevents her from speaking audibly.

"How are you?" I ask.

"Fine" her lips say.

"Do you want to work with flowers today?"

"Yes," she nods with a smile.

I have with me a jar of water filled with an assortment of flowers I picked in the garden that morning. I set the jar on the tray in front of Ahuva. She surveys the flowers as I slowly turn the jar. I give Ahuva a small plastic cup (like an applesauce container), into which she carefully places a green flower-arranging sponge. I add water to the cup so that the sponge is saturated. Then Ahuva begins thoughtfully selecting flowers, one at a time, from the jar. She meticulously removes any lower leaves from the stems and firmly (sometimes a bit too firmly) inserts the stem of the flower into the sponge. I talk to her throughout —about the flower she selected, what it's called, what color it is. If the stem appears too long, she will hold it out to me so that I can prune it. Ahuva generally chooses the pink or red flowers first. She also likes purple. One day, she surprised me by filling the cup with yellow flowers before picking the first pink one.

Ahuva applies herself to the task of selecting the flowers and placing them in the sponge with such concentration that she occasionally forgets to breathe. The alarm on the pulse oxygen monitor on the wall over her head sounds, and one can see the oxygen saturation number go down into the 80s. I gently place my hand on her shoulder and say, "Ahuva, breathe deeply, breathe deeply" while demonstrating exaggerated deep breaths. Sometimes a nurse or an aide, summoned by the alarm, arrives before Ahuva can get her oxygen saturation numbers back up to the desired level. The alarm also sounds when the hose from the oxygen pump disconnects from the tube in her throat. I simply reconnect the hose, her pulse oxygen rises to a normal level, the alarm ceases, and we go on.

The bouquets Ahuva makes are always cheery and festive. She smiles with pride, gazing at her creations. I usually take a picture of her grinning as she admires the small flower arrangement. Occasionally, she asks me to give the bouquet to the staff at the desk on the unit.

On the wall next to Ahuva's bed hangs a large photo collage, printed on canvas, with dozens of photos of her with computer-generated emojis, being embraced by family, friends, and staff of the rehab center. In each one, Ahuva's large round face beams. Next to that is a poster of animal photos. Photos of brightly colored flowers adorn the wall opposite her bed. And, tucked into the sill of the window next to her bed (whose shades are always drawn) is a pile of plush stuffed animals. Ahuva means "beloved," and the notes and greetings taped to the wall next to her bed are testimony to how beloved she is by the staff at the hospital.

Occasionally, when I arrive for my session with Ahuva, one of the aides on the unit is spoon-feeding her a breakfast of soft foods—oatmeal or porridge, yogurt, and pureed fruit. I wait until she's finished eating before starting our session. I am surprised that she can arrange flowers but is unable to feed herself. I ask her mother about this. She tells me that Ahuva can feed herself but that the staff are concerned that she might choke on her food. Perhaps, they reason, it is faster for a staff member to feed her than to have someone sit with her while she feeds herself.

Ahuva, who is in her early 60s, was born with mild developmental delays and cognitive deficits. She also suffers from diabetes and a host of related medical conditions. Despite, or perhaps because of, her difficulties, Ahuva's parents, who also have a grown son and adult grandchildren, doted on her. They afforded her every opportunity to optimize her potential. After they retired, they traveled with her extensively in Europe and around the world. Then, five years ago, Ahuva was found unresponsive in her bed. She had fallen into a diabetic coma. This resulted in severe respiratory damage and exacerbated her other medical conditions. It also led to a deterioration in her cognitive abilities. After a time in intensive care, she emerged from the coma, but continues to be dependent on the ventilator. She has been at the rehab center for almost five years, and it appears that this will be her permanent home.

During the fourth COVID wave, the ventilator unit, like many of the inpatient units at the hospital, was under quarantine. However, therapists were allowed to enter the unit provided they "suited up" in a disposable gown, N95 mask, plastic face shield over the mask, and rubber gloves before entering. I suited up, as required, and entered the unit. Between the N95 mask, which I was not accustomed to wearing, and the face shield, I found it somewhat difficult to breathe. Then I stopped for a moment and thought about the people who reside in the unit I had just entered. How could I complain about a few minutes of stuffiness when all day, every day, for the rest of their lives, these people struggle for breath, coughing violently when the ventilator tube needs to be suctioned, or not able to breathe at all when the tube disconnects from the port in their throats?

I regularly meet with Ahuva at 10 a.m., precisely the hour her parents arrive to visit her every day. The two, both nearing 90, shuffle slowly into the unit, each leaning on a cane. They greet Ahuva lovingly, as one would a young child, with her pet name, Ahuvela. They also exchange "good mornings" with the wife of the patient at the far end of the room. Ahuva's parents often sit in the hallway and read the paper while I work with their daughter, but occasionally, her mother sits on the bed, and we chat while Ahuva attends to her gardening tasks. I was told that her parents sold their house and moved to be closer to the facility where their daughter lives.

Another activity Ahuva enjoyed consists of picking lavender leaves from their stems so that they can be dried and used to make sachets. I pick fresh sprigs of lavender from the bushes at the entrance to the rehab center and bring them to Ahuva. She holds the stem in one hand and, with the other, meticulously picks off the leaves, one at a time, in order from the bottom to the top, placing them in a container with the leaves she plucked in previous sessions. Ahuva hands me the bare stem and eagerly takes another to strip off its leaves. I once mentioned to an occupational therapist who also works with Ahuva that I try to vary the activities I undertake with her, as picking leaves off lavender stems week after week seemed rather boring. She replied, "It may seem that way to you, but Ahuva really enjoys it. She looks forward to your bringing her the lavender branches."

Her words gave me pause. I need to be vigilant and not project my feelings onto my patients. What to me would be a tedious, repetitive task is a diversion and a productive activity for Ahuva. She spends most of each day having things done to her or for her. She cannot dress herself; she is dressed. She cannot feed herself; she is fed. She watches TV and listens to music. She is the passive recipient of the stimuli that enliven her day. Ahuva's sessions with me are among the few active breaks in her routine. Whether arranging flowers in a cup or plucking leaves off a stem, Ahuva is acting on her environment. She is creating something with her own hands. She is making decisions, even if the choice is only which leaf to pull off next. She examines each stem to be sure she has removed every tiny leaf. She looks at the bare stem admiringly before handing it back to me. At the end of our session, Ahuva likes to reach her hand into the container to mix and feel the drying leaves and see how much work she has done and how much fuller the container is than it was when I brought it to her.

Once we have accumulated enough leaves and they are completely dry, I bring Ahuva small tuille bags. She fills the bags with dried lavender leaves and, with a look of pride, pulls the tiny satin ribbons to close the bags. I tie the ribbons in a knot. These fragrant sachets can be used to keep lingerie smelling fresh. Ahuva's mother takes some of the bags to give as gifts. Others

are sold to patients, staff, and visitors to raise money for the garden. Ahuva obviously derives great satisfaction from every step of the production of the sachets. It is a sad irony, however, that she cannot appreciate the enchanting fragrance of the lavender sachets she so meticulously prepares. She has no sense of smell.

It occurred to me that for a bit of variety, I could bring Ahuva an assortment of plant materials—colorful dried bougain-villea leaves, seeds, dried beans, acorns, pistachio shells and the like—for her to use to make a collage. Ahuva responded enthu-siastically when I first proposed this activity. She readily under-

stood the task and began meticulously squeezing dots of glue on the cardboard, and thoughtfully selecting materials to glue. It took her a few sessions to complete a collage, but the result was an original, artistically designed creation. I photographed each of Ahuva's collages to share with my colleagues, who were impressed with her creativity and aesthetic sensibility. We hung the finished collages next to her bed, in place of some of the animal and flower photos which previously adorned her wall.

Unfortunately, with time, Ahuva's ability to do the gluing and pasting waned. She was slower to respond and seemed to have great difficulty selecting items to glue to the board. She would sometimes sit motionless for ten to fifteen minutes, staring at the array of seeds and leaves I brought her, unable to decide what to do. I would cajole and encourage her, usually to no avail. Sometimes, I would select a nut shell or fruit pit, place it in her hand, and suggest she glue it here or there on the cardboard. There were days she took a bit more initiative, but for the most part, I observed a steady deterioration in Ahuva's energy, alertness, and "executive function."

I alternated the collages with flower arranging, hoping the colorful flowers that used to delight her would stimulate her to be more active. Alas, here, too, Ahuva was mostly passive. When she didn't choose a flower to put into the arrangement, I would choose one for her, put it in her hand, and try to persuade her to put the stem in the sponge. Most times, she eventually responded, but, while she used to make three or more arrangements in a session, she now could barely complete one, and that with a great deal of help from me.

At such times, I struggle to suppress my urge to "just do it for her". With difficulty I have learned to be patient. If Ahuva won't pick up a flower on her own, I put it in her hand. If cajoling her to insert the flower into the sponge doesn't work, I gently take her hand with the flower in it and help her reach out to put it in. I need to remind her to release her hand once the flower is in place. I am increasingly able to say to myself, it's okay if she only puts one flower in the vase before drifting off again. At least she has used her hands.

Ahuva's parents were very concerned about the obvious decline in her alertness, energy, and activity. They felt it was in part due to the medication she was receiving. However, it seems more likely that this change represented a deterioration in her underlying condition, which they have difficulty accepting. Still, there are days when Ahuva is a bit more responsive and more active and seems to take pride and pleasure in her work with flowers and plants.

Watching Ahuva's steady decline left me feeling sad, and particularly sorry for her parents, who had invested so much in trying to maintain the quality of their unfortunate daughter's life. Sometimes when I entered the room, Ahuva was sound asleep in her wheelchair as her mother sat, dozing, on the edge of the bed, holding her hand. I tried to rouse Ahuva, and in the process woke her mother. The two of us would then try to get Ahuva to open her eyes. On those occasions, I felt that my visit was more for her mother's benefit than for Ahuva. When we didn't succeed in waking Ahuva, I would chat with her mother as I fashioned a small bouquet. Her mother clearly appreciated the flowers and the companionship.

I have learned more from my work with patients in the ventilator unit than I have from any other group of patients. Tailoring activities to match their abilities challenges my creativity and imagination. And, unlike with patients who can speak, it is at times difficult to gauge their response to my presence. Sometimes it is only an eye blink or a hint of a smile.

Chapter 4

A Cooking Lesson

Mazal was different from the other patients I encountered on the ventilator unit. She was in the process of being weaned from the ventilator. She would sit in a chair still tethered to her vent but could use her hands and was even beginning to stand and take a few steps. She was able to remove the tube, cover her trach hole, and speak audible words. Before I started my internship, one of the gardening therapists learned that Mazal loved to cook. Mazal told us that she had a wonderful recipe for pita with za'atar, an herb used in Middle Eastern cooking. But first, we needed the za'atar in a usable form. The therapist therefore started bringing za'atar branches to Mazal, so that she could remove the leaves from the stems. Mazal would dexterously pull each leaf off the stem and put the leaves in a container. She had surprising energy.

Za'atar is not actually a specific plant but a mixture of herbs and spices whose main ingredient, often called za'atar, is an herb closely related to oregano. It is native to the Middle East and has been over-harvested, so wild "za'atar" is now a protected species. However, the plant can be easily grown in a garden or a pot.

The za'atar leaves need to be dried so that they can be crushed and turned into powder. Each week, I took the leaves Mazal had separated from the stems and spread them on paper towels to dry. The following week, I brought the drying leaves back to Mazal to ask her whether they were dry enough to be crushed. No, they needed more time. I also brought her more branches to pick. Week after week, we followed this routine. (All the while, we also made small bouquets from the cut flowers I brought her.) One day, when I arrived at her bedside, Mazal complained that she wasn't feeling well. But her face lit up when she saw and smelled the rose I had brought to the unit. Despite her headache, she showed even greater delight when she saw the other flowers I had with me. Then she asked to see the za'atar. "It's ready," she announced. "It's time to buy the sesame seeds and the sumac needed for the recipe," she instructed me excitedly.

We made plans to meet in the occupational therapy kitchen for our session the following week. This was not as simple as it sounds. While she was being weaned from the ventilator, Mazal continued to need supplemental oxygen. We therefore had to arrange for a wheelchair with an oxygen tank and a volunteer to wheel her to the kitchen and back at the designated time. When the big day came, another therapist and I met Mazal in the kitchen. We had brought the dried za'atar and a book of plants and recipes to give her as a gift. Using a mortar and pestle, Mazal ground the dried za'atar leaves until they were just the right consistency. We put the ground za'atar in a container. The volunteer wheeled Mazal back to the unit. Next week we would meet in the kitchen again, and Mazal would show us how to bake the pita.

Unfortunately, when the long-awaited baking day came, I was unable to be at the hospital. I was very disappointed, but

Mazal's Recipe for Za'atar Pita

2 Tbs sugar
A pinch of salt
2 cups water
1 kg. flour
1 cube yeast

In a mixer, mix the above ingredients
Leave dough in mixer to rise
Cut dough into 12 balls—roll them out flat
Let rise again
Put on tray for oven

Make za'atar mixture:
Olive oil
Dried, crushed za'atar
50 gm sesame seeds
Salt
Lemon salt
Sumac

Spread za'atar mixture on dough
Bake at 180 degrees Celsius (350F) for 20 min+,
or until browm

we could not disappoint Mazal. My colleague met her in the kitchen with all the ingredients she had specified in her recipe. With great enthusiasm, she mixed the dough, let it rise, cut it into balls, and rolled them flat, letting them rise a second time. While the dough was rising, Mazal mixed the za'atar with the other seasonings. She spread the za'atar mixture on the flattened dough balls after they had risen and put them in the oven to bake. I understand that Mazal was proud and delighted at the sight and the smell of the baking bread. I so wish I could have been there. Mazal gave my colleague one of the pitas to give me. It was delicious!!

Perhaps instructing us to make the za'atar pita brought Mazal back to her time as preschool teacher, before she fell ill with the muscular disease that led to her long stay at the rehab hospital. In addition, any time the long-term patients leave the tiny circumference of their lives in the hospital, whether to go up to the garden or the occupational therapy kitchen, their world expands.

The following week, I told her that the pita was scrumptious and how sorry I was that I couldn't be there when she baked it. We talked at some length about it—she was still basking in delight. She then turned the conversation to her impending discharge from the hospital. She was excited and grateful to be leaving the rehab facility. As it happened, she wasn't exactly going home. Instead, she was embarking on a new life. Mazal and her husband had separated during her long hospitalization. She was looking forward to moving to a new residence with a caregiver to assist her.

Chapter 5

An Avocado Tree Four Stories Tall

.

When I arrive at the rehab center in the morning, I go up to the garden, don my olive-green gardening apron emblazoned with the rehab center logo, and begin to prepare my materials for the patients I plan to meet during the day. If I will be going down to the units, I put the materials on a wheeled cart, which I take down in the elevator to the unit where my patients reside. On days when I run a "group," I try to get an idea from the occupational therapist or the activities coordinator on the unit how many patients she anticipates will participate in the group that day. It's always just a guess. I once led a group in which the participants were named Abraham, Isaac, Jacob, and Vladimir. In the complex medical unit, the number of patients in a group may vary from zero to eight, depending on who is not feeling well, who had to leave for medical reasons, and who is no longer in the unit.

A gardening therapy "group" can have many meanings. Some groups—such as those of outpatients or healthier inpatients —involve multiple participants who interact with one another verbally while also working on various gardening projects together or in parallel. They typically sit around a table to facilitate face-to-face conversation and so the therapist can see everyone—and vice versa—simultaneously.

As many of the patients in the complex medical unit either cannot speak because they have tracheostomies, cognitive impairment or neurological conditions limiting their speech, there is rarely verbal interaction among the participants. Rather, the session resembles "parallel play" among young children. Everyone seated around the table is engaged in an activity—either the same activity as others or something different—but working at their own pace while I move from one to another to assist, guide, and encourage them. I also try to chat with each of the patients. If a family member is visiting a patient in the group, I will often enlist their help to work with that patient so I can spend more time helping others.

The common room in the unit is a hive of activity. In addition to "my" patients seated around the table, each in their wheelchair, often with an oxygen tank attached at the back, other more severely incapacitated patients are parked in their wheelchairs around the periphery of the room, sleeping, mumbling, or shouting out. Nurses, orderlies, therapists, and cleaning staff cut through the space on their way to or from the patient rooms that surround the common area. Though it doesn't sound like the optimal therapeutic environment, I have learned to tune out the surrounding chaos, and my patients appear to do likewise.

Once I have a sense of who will be participating that day—and it's only a sense, as the actual number of patients can change at the last minute—I determine what activities are appropriate for each individual and what supplies I will need to load on the cart. I fill plastic containers with soil. I bring empty pots (of the size appropriate to what we will be planting), spades, and soup spoons (many patients lack the strength to lift even a plastic spade full of potting soil), small plastic watering cans, saucers, etc. Then I go out to the garden to collect cuttings, or I put small jars of seeds or containers of bulbs on the cart. I usually also cut colorful flowers, which I put in a jar full of water to serve as a centerpiece on the worktable in the unit. If the patients whom I expect to participate in the group on a particular day have seedlings or cuttings in the greenhouse, I check to see whether their plants have grown or their seeds have sprouted and bring them to show or transplant to larger pots.

The trip down to the unit, only two floors below the garden, is itself often a therapeutic experience. I roll my loaded cart to the elevator, push the down button, and wait. Because this is a rehab hospital, the elevator doors are programmed to remain open for a long time on each floor so that patients in wheelchairs or on crutches have time to exit and enter. Since there are only two elevators in the building, they tend to be crowded and stop on every floor. When it finally arrives, I try to squeeze myself and the loaded cart into the car among the patients in wheelchairs, the walkers, and other carts already on board. Invariably, patients, staff, and visitors in the elevator comment on the flowers and plants that fill my cart. Many ask if they can have a plant or a flower. Some ask if they can buy a plant. Not infrequently, patients will ask me if I have cannabis. "I'm sorry, I don't." When I explain that I am taking these plants to a unit for gardening therapy, patients ask me how they can arrange to visit the garden or sign up for gardening therapy. The cart full of plants and flowers invariably brings a smile to the faces of anyone riding in the elevator, whether they are patients, volunteers pushing wheelchairs, or delivery men with their huge carts of adult diapers.

One day I arrived at the complex medical unit with my cart stocked for all contingencies, as the occupational therapist wasn't sure who might participate. It turned out that there weren't any patients able to participate in a group, but she introduced me to Alon, a new patient in the unit, in the hope that he might want to work with me. Alon sat in his motorized wheelchair. He had thinning salt and pepper hair and a few days' growth of stubble on his face. His torso was short, and his hospital pajama top, partially buttoned, barely covered his stocky, hairy chest and belly. I immediately noticed the stump where his left leg used to be. With a distressed and angry expression on his face, Alon replied in the negative. The therapist asked if he was in pain. Grimacing, he revealed the four teeth in his mouth (two upper and two lower with huge spaces between them). He said he was in terrible pain. He was miserable. "It's unbearable. A prison would be better than this place." Then he said snidely, "And you think working with plants will help!! I need to talk with a social worker. I can't stand this. Plants??!!" The occupational therapist said she would try to find his social worker. In the meantime, she suggested to me other patients on the unit whom I might visit in bed.

Then, out of the corner of my eye, I noticed that Alon had wheeled himself to my laden cart, which I had left in a corner of the room. He was surveying the cuttings and equipment I had brought. I saw him reach down from his wheelchair to take a small flowerpot from the bottom shelf of the cart and use it to scoop up soil from the container of potting mix on the cart. I motioned to the occupational therapist to look. We winked at each other over our COVID masks. I walked over to Alon just as he helped himself to a succulent cutting and deftly planted it in the soil in the pot he'd filled. He took another one and planted it in the same pot. I suggested he might want a larger pot. "No, this is fine," he said as he planted a third succulent cutting in the same pot, creating a charming "succulent cocktail." I smiled at him and said, "How lovely! Well done!" He grabbed another small pot, filled it with soil, and in one swift move, planted a coleus cutting and then another in the second pot. "You seem to know what you're doing," I observed. I asked him if he had a garden.

"Of course," he said, with a slight smile lifting the corners of his mouth, again revealing those four canine teeth. And the floodgates opened.

Alon told me that he had grown up in a town in the north of Israel. Before the holiday of *Tu B'Shvat*, a Jewish celebration of trees and fruit, which usually falls in January, his mother would take him to the market to buy broad beans. They would spread the beans on damp towels, and when they had sprouted, plant them. In short order, the plants would grow tall and produce beans. He also explained that you can cut pieces of old potatoes and plant them in soil, and, in about three months, when the foliage has dried, you have potatoes to harvest. I told him that I did that here with a patient on this unit, and I cooked and ate the potatoes we harvested. He further reminisced about the row of corn stalks he planted and grew as a child.

And then, with great pride, Alon recounted how he had sprouted an avocado pit in water. When it grew roots and the stem started to emerge, he planted it in a pot, into which he had put orange peels as compost. I nodded as he described rooting the pit in water and told him I'd never heard of using oranges as compost but that it sounded like a good idea. He said the avocado plant thrived and eventually became a tree four stories tall. Perhaps it is not a coincidence that his name, Alon, means oak tree. In the fourth year[3], that one tree yielded 50 kilos of avocados[4]!"

"Wow!" I said with genuine amazement. I asked him how they picked the fruit from such a tall tree. He explained that they used ladders for the lower branches and beat the tree with a stick to get the fruit down from the higher branches. "Wouldn't that cause the avocados to be damaged when they hit the ground?" I asked naively.

"No, you pick them when they are still hard and can withstand the fall," he replied.

"Of course!" It dawned on me.

Just as odors are extremely evocative and, as with Proust, often stimulate recollections of one's past, so are plants, even those with no fragrance. Time after time, as happened with Alon, a patient will plant cuttings or seeds and begin to reminisce

---

3   The Bible (Leviticus 19:23) prohibits eating the fruit produced during the first three years after the tree was planted. The years since the planting of a fruit tree are counted in a fashion analogous to the way the age of a thoroughbred racehorse is determined. The birthday of all thoroughbreds is January 1 of the year the horse was born. Similarly, the age of a fruit tree is counted from Rosh Hashanah (the Jewish New Year) of the year the tree was planted.

about their childhood gardening experiences. Such memories are generally positive and bring a smile to the patient's face as they recount stories of harvesting vegetables at the home of a favorite uncle or planting herbs with their mother.

I told Alon that we had a garden on the roof of the hospital and asked if he'd be interested in seeing it. He wanted to know what we have there. I told him that we don't have avocado trees, but we do have some fruit trees —Chinese orange, pitango, pomegranate, fig, and grape vines. He told me that one can grow a pomegranate tree from a branch. Then, with a big, mostly toothless grin, he described how, after pruning the trees down to a meter high, he added the cut pomegranate, peach, and plum branches to the fire on which he roasted meat. It not only added fragrance but imparted a delectable flavor to the meat. People would ask him where he bought his unusually delicious meat.

Again, I asked if he would like to visit the garden on the roof. I told him that we had flowers, vegetables, an herb garden, and a succulent corner. I suggested he might like to come up and look around just to enjoy the fresh air and a change of scenery. He considered it. We tentatively agreed that the following week he would meet me in the garden. Unfortunately, the following week, Alon was not at the rehab center. I was distressed to learn that he had been taken to the hospital. The poor man! My disappointment may have been greater than my concern for him. I had so eagerly looked forward to showing him around the garden and giving him the chance to demonstrate more of his skill with plants.

My encounter with Alon ranks as one of my most gratifying days as a gardening therapist. Perhaps it's a close second to the day Mina told me, on seeing that all her cherry tomatoes had sprouted, that she felt like a woman in the delivery room. Both cases speak volumes about the therapeutic power of plants. Reflecting on this, I realize that my role is less "therapist" than "medium." I bring the patients to the garden (or bring the garden to the patients) and let the plants work their magic.

---

4   Avocados have become an important commercial crop in Israel. According to one of the most prominent avocado growers in Israel, avocados are the most profitable legal produce in the country. Israel exports approximately 45 percent of its avocado crop.

Chapter 6

Confronting Death

Sasha was a Bukharan Jew. The Bukharans are an ancient ethno-re-ligious group who come from a region of what is now Uzbekistan. Their traditional language is a mixture of Hebrew and Persian, though most speak Russian. Beginning in 1972, large numbers of Bukharan Jews migrated to the West. Most of those who remained left Uzbekistan after the fall of the Soviet Union twenty years later. Many came to Israel. I do not know when Sasha's family emigrated, but his mother tongue was Russian.

Each time I entered the common room of the complex medical unit, I saw him there. A large man with a black velvet *kippah* (skullcap) on his balding head, he had a trach tube protruding from his throat. The oxygen pump at the back of his wheelchair was plugged into an electric outlet in the wall behind him. He was usually watching something on a tablet propped on the table in front of him. Possibly because of his poor health and his weight, he looked much older than his 65 years.

I wheeled my cart full of gardening supplies and plants toward Sasha and asked if he wanted to garden. With his finger, he covered the opening of the trach tube and said, "Okay," a reluctant smile spreading over his ruddy face. He slowly folded the tablet shut. He let me help him put on an apron. He usually wanted rubber gloves on his hands before he started to work with soil. I struggled to fit the tight disposable gloves over his large, swollen fingers.

Every time I approached Sasha at the beginning of a session, he gave me the sense that I was disturbing him by taking him away from his tablet. Nevertheless, once he got started, his enthusiasm and energy were irrepressible. Whatever the task, he worked independently, quickly, and competently. He knew just what needed to be done. Some days, he planted succulent cuttings. Other days, he expertly repotted flowers into larger pots. He accomplished a lot in an hour. When he finished planting what I had initially given to him, he pointed proudly to the pots he'd filled and asked me for more plants, pots, and soil, or whatever the materials were that he was working with that day. Sasha's zeal for gardening was a surprising contrast with the passiveness and indifference he displayed at the beginning of each session.

The first time I came to the unit, I demonstrated to the group how one can grow potatoes from the eyes of an old potato. During successive weeks, I would bring Sasha the bag in which we planted the potatoes so that he could add soil to cover the new green growth. After a couple of months of adding soil weekly, we let the stems and leaves grow out of the top of the bag.

When, a few weeks later, the leaves had withered, I brought the bag to Sasha so that he could harvest the potatoes we hoped to find in the soil at the bottom of the bag. He dug down and, with a look of triumph in his light brown eyes, pulled out a handful of small round potatoes. He emptied the bag and out poured a dozen more small spuds with the remaining soil. Sasha's full face beamed. I asked him if he wanted the potatoes. He said, "I can't do anything with them here."

"Would it be alright for me to take them?" I asked.

"Why not?" he replied. I took our lovely new potatoes home, cooked them, and served them with dinner. They were particularly delicious.

From November through February, in addition to other materials, I brought a variety of bulbs—hyacinths, narcissus, crocuses, freesias, anemones, and irises —to the unit. The rehab center receives a variety of donations, in kind and in money, from generous individuals and organizations around the world. Among these contributions are cases of tulips and other spring flower bulbs sent by Evangelical Christians in Holland. The packages of bulbs are labeled with the names of individual donors. We photograph the hands of the patients planting and tending the bulbs to send with our thank-you notes to the benefactors. Bulb flowers used to be very rare in Israel. Now they are available in flower shops, but most are either imported or grown in pots under controlled conditions, as the winters are not cold enough here for the bulbs to produce roots in the ground. However, they can be "forced" by putting them in the refrigerator before planting.

The task for the patients was to fill pots with soil, make holes in the soil for the bulbs, and plant a bulb in each hole with the pointed end up. For many of the patients in the group, inserting the bulb right side up was a challenge. While I usually try not to insist that they plant in a certain way, if the bulbs are planted upside down (with the flatter side up), they will not grow. I gently try to correct some of the patients. However, when dealing with those whose dexterity is very limited, I simply let them insert the bulbs as best they could and replanted them in the proper direction when I got back to the garden.

Sasha needed no correction. Each week, I brought different flower bulbs. He planted dozens of bulbs of all kinds, each inserted pointed side up in the center of its pot. In the case of the smaller bulbs, he would plant more than one in each pot. Each pot was labeled with an orange tag with Sasha's name, the date, and the kind of bulb it contained. When I arrived in the garden in the morning, I checked the progress of Sasha's bulbs and brought with me to the unit any pots whose bulbs had sprouted. Sasha smiled broadly when he saw the green shoots emerging from his bulbs. Eventually, the bulbs bloomed. I was delighted

to fill my cart with the colorful and fragrant hyacinths and freesia and the delicately intricate irises.

Sasha didn't talk much, as he had to cover his trach tube in order to speak audibly. Consequently, we never had a real conversation; we exchanged only a word or two here and there. But he communicated very clearly with his facial expressions and hand gestures. There was no doubt when he wanted more material to work with. And it was perfectly clear that he found great satisfaction in seeing the glorious product of his efforts.

One day, Sasha wasn't in the common room when I came in with my cart. He had been taken to the hospital. A few weeks later, I learned he had died. This was my first experience of the death of a patient. I was struck by the absence of any mention or discussion of his passing with the other patients in the group, people from the unit who had sat with him in the common room day in and day out, in some cases for many years. His seat in the corner, where his oxygen pump could be plugged into the wall, remained empty. I was troubled that there was nothing done in his memory.

Some weeks later, I was working individually in the garden with a patient from the complex medical unit. She suddenly asked me, "What happened to that man who used to sit at the table in the corner and work with you?"

"Do you mean Sasha?"

"Yes," she replied.

I told her that he had died a few weeks previously. She was shocked. Her face dropped and her eyes filled with tears. "He was such a cheerful, good-natured man," I said. Adding, "I was so sad to hear he had died."

"Why didn't anyone say anything? Why didn't anyone tell me?" she continued.

I told her I had wondered the same thing. I asked some of the veteran therapists about this. They didn't offer a satisfactory response. "We just don't talk about a patient's demise," they said.

People just disappear. Their empty beds are soon filled

with a new patient, and the rhythm of the unit goes on without missing a beat. I don't mean to suggest that the staff on the unit are in any way insensitive or uncaring or that they don't develop attachments to the patients, some of whom reside on the unit for decades. Rather, there is simply no discussion with other patients of the demise of one of their number.

I took up this issue with the spiritual counselor on the staff of the center. She appreciated my concerns, explaining that the death of a patient affects three distinct populations: the staff, the other patients, and the family of the deceased. Her work has mostly been with dying patients and their families, when they want her help. She noted that the staff generally prefer to go immediately back to their routine. But she acknowledged that something should be done with the patients in the complex medical unit to mark the passing of a fellow patient. I told her another patient had asked me why nothing had been said or done when Sasha died. I also suggested that patients in that unit, who are generally quite sick and may feel their own death approaching, may be distressed to think that after they are gone, nothing will be said or done in their memory in the place they called home, often for many years. She agreed.

Sasha was a widower. His wife died when they were both young. They were childless. He had several brothers. After Sasha took ill, one of his brothers became his guardian and took over his assets, installing his own son in Sasha's apartment. Sasha wanted to leave the hospital but had nowhere to go since his nephew was living in his apartment. He lived more than a decade at the rehab hospital. He loved the activities at the hospital, and the staff spoiled him. For Sasha, I later learned, the hospital was his family. How sad to pass away and not to be mourned by one's family.

Gardening forces us to confront death. The life cycle of annual flowers and most vegetables is short. A seed sprouts, grows, flowers, bears fruit or seeds, and dies, often within a matter of months. In addition, seeds we plant often fail to germinate, and many times, seedlings don't flourish. Or a thriving plant is suddenly attacked by disease, mold, or insects. It withers and dies. But sadness for that loss may be offset by the fruit the plant bears and the potential for new life it represents. This reality has therapeutic value in many settings. It can help patients deal with loss and bereavement, leading them to see that death and loss are part of the natural order, that nature has built-in recovery mechanisms—in plants and in people. Nothing was ever done to memorialize Sasha. But it may be that in a place like the complex medical unit, where death looms everywhere, people don't need to dwell on it.

Chapter 7

Rivka

Rivka sat in her wheelchair in the common room. Her head, covered with thick, tousled gray hair, rested in her hands, facing down. A lanky woman probably in her late 70s, she didn't look up when I approached her. One of the aides on the unit told me that she was often unresponsive. I tried a different tack. I brought her the jar of flowers I'd cut in the garden that morning, held it in front of her face, and softly said, "Rivka." She immediately picked up her head, reached for the flowers with both hands, and began exclaiming in a hoarse, throaty voice, "Oh, oh, flowers, beautiful!" "Flowers, wow!" "How beautiful!" She pulled the jar close to her face so she could smell the flowers. "Wow," she cried again. The occupational therapist was amazed when I described to her Rivka's enthusiastic response to the flowers.

Building on this success, on subsequent visits to the unit I brought Rivka pots, which she filled with soil. She planted coleus cuttings, herbs, and succulents. She worked with energy and enthusiasm, always marveling at the beauty of the plants. After a few such positive sessions, I asked if she would like to come up to the roof garden and work with me individually. She readily agreed. The next week, a volunteer wheeled Rivka to the garden. On first seeing the garden, Rivka shouted out with delight, "How beautiful! How beautiful!" As we toured the garden, Rivka smiled broadly and exclaimed with wonder at the flowers, fruits, and vegetables.

I prepared a project for her—planting a succulent "cocktail" in a large shallow pot. I frequently use succulents in my work with patients. The dazzling array of shapes and configurations, textures and colors of these sturdy plants makes them interesting for patients to work with. They are attractive alone or in combination, in what we refer to as a succulent "cocktail." Their "fur," prickly spines, raised bumps, and smooth fleshy "leaves" provide tactile stimulation, particularly for visually impaired patients. Succulents are easy to propagate. Cuttings root quickly in even the poorest soil. Many species multiply on their own, spawning "baby" plants from their base or their extremities. These can be removed and planted. Under auspicious conditions, when there is enough rain, succulents flower, and their flowers produce seeds, which can be planted.

In addition to their visual and tactile attraction, succulents offer therapeutic lessons. These plants have adapted to extreme and generally inhospitable conditions. They have evolved to thrive in deserts and other arid regions. For example, their plump leaves store water to sustain them during extended periods of drought. Many have needles or spines instead of leaves so that water does not evaporate quickly. Thorns and prickles also protect them from predatory animals. Indeed "Sabra" is a term used to refer to a native Israeli, as the cactus fruit's prickly exterior and sweet interior are thought to describe the Israeli

character. Discussing the adaptive mechanisms of succulents can help patients think about their own adaptation to their newfound limitations.

Rivka filled the pot with soil mixed with compost and selected succulent cuttings, which she planted in an aesthetically pleasing arrangement. I was hugely impressed at her dexterity, initiative, and concentration.

The following week, I prepared another project for her in the garden. However, when she arrived, she said she was tired and didn't feel like working. I wheeled her around the garden, pointing out flowers that had just bloomed, but she lacked the enthusiasm of her first visit and asked me to take her downstairs.

When I came to the unit the next week, Rivka was in bed, looking weak and tired. She perked up a bit when I showed her the flowers I'd brought. I also gave her hyacinths and freesia to smell, which brought a smile to her face and a sparkle to her blue eyes. I left a small bouquet in a cup on the stand next to her bed. Sadly, this was the last time I saw Rivka. She contracted COVID and died shortly thereafter.

Chapter 8

A Gift from Beyond the Grave

In early January 2021, there was an outbreak of COVID in the complex medical unit. Although I had had my first COVID vaccination two weeks prior, I caught COVID and was sick, though mercifully not dangerously so, for about two weeks. When I received the positive diagnosis, I contacted some of my colleagues and learned that they, too, had been infected. Several patients and staff on the unit had also contracted the disease. After I recovered, I was ready to go back to work but was told that the unit was in quarantine. It was another month before the unit was released from quarantine and I was permitted to return.

When I returned to the hospital in February 2021 and went down to the unit to work with my group of patients, I was shocked and deeply saddened to learn that three of them had succumbed to COVID. Granted they were old and suffered from background diseases, but because the last time I'd seen them they were relatively healthy, the news of their passing was particularly upsetting. I also noticed that the population of the unit had changed since before the COVID outbreak. The new patients tended to be sicker and less able to participate in group gardening activities around the table. Most were bedridden, and I visited and worked with them individually in their rooms.

Yitzhak was one of the few new patients on the unit who sat in his wheelchair at the table in the common room. Dressed in hospital pajamas (some patients wear their own clothes), he had a slight build, gray hair, sparkling gray-green eyes, and an impish expression. He sometimes slipped sideways in his chair and needed a boost to return to an upright position. I introduced myself and asked if he wanted to smell the herbs I had brought with me on the cart. "Yes," he whispered, with a smile on his face and a glint in his eyes.

He held each sprig under his nose, inhaled deeply, and tried to guess which herb it was. We chatted about how the herbs are used—some for tea, some for seasoning in cooking, some for sachets. "Herbs revive the spirit," he said, grinning. I showed him the flowers on my cart. He took the jar and smelled the flowers. Given his enthusiasm for the flowers, I asked if he would like me to make a small bouquet in a cup, which he could put on the stand next to his bed. He appeared delighted.

Yitzhak welcomed me warmly when he saw me enter the common room the following week with my cart full of plants and flowers. Once again, he smelled herbs and tried to identify them. "Would you make me a bouquet to take back to my room?" he asked shyly. I was delighted to. At the end of the session, he thanked me for the visit with a broad smile.

At our next session, Yitzhak was ready to "work." With

great zest, he filled eight pots with potting soil and meticulously planted a succulent cutting in each pot. Although he protested at first that the watering can was too heavy for him to lift without help, after I initially supported the can, he watered them all himself. I was thrilled to see him work independently and energetically. He seemed stronger than he had during my previous visits. His face expressed his pride at his accomplishment. I had the sense that if there'd been time, he'd have gone on planting as long as the supply of pots, soil, and plants lasted.

On another occasion, he briskly filled six pots with soil, separated cuttings, planted, and watered them without any assistance. "This reminds me of a time when I was asked to help plant trees for the army," he told me.

"Really? Tell me more about that," I replied.

"I was a truck driver for the army, and they needed extra help planting trees at a base in Sde Boker [a kibbutz in the south of the country]." He continued, "They asked all the truck drivers to help." Clearly, this was an event he remembered fondly, and he mentioned it again during subsequent meetings.

One day, I brought Yitzhak wads of cotton from one of the cotton plants in the garden. I showed him that the cotton contained seeds. He massaged the soft cotton balls in his fingers. "I can feel the seeds," he told me. I asked him to remove the seeds from the fluffy cotton. Then, he filled trays of small pots with soil, carefully made a hole in the soil with his finger, and planted a seed in each hole. He meticulously covered the seeds with soil and watered all the pots. I put an orange tag with his name, the date, and the word "cotton" in each tray and took them up to the greenhouse.

A couple of weeks later, Yitzhak was seated at the table but complained that he was in a lot of pain and didn't have his usual energy. Nonetheless, he spent a half hour filling pots and preparing and planting cuttings. I then showed him that all the cotton seeds had sprouted. He was thrilled.

After a few weeks, I again brought the cotton seedlings

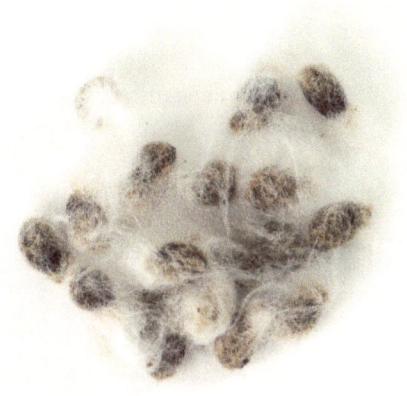

down from the greenhouse. It was time to transplant them into larger pots. With great joy and efficiency, Yitzhak filled six large pots with soil. He tenderly removed the delicate plants from their small pots and placed them in the hole he'd made in the soil in each of the larger pots. He added soil to each pot, as needed, and watered them. His face glowed and his eyes twinkled. Yitzhak's spirit and gentleness moved me deeply. I always looked forward to working with him.

      The next time I saw Yitzhak, he was in his room in bed. We chatted a bit. Together, we made a small flower arrangement in a cup, which I left next to his bed. Two weeks later, I again found Yitzhak in bed. This time he appeared feeble. We spoke briefly. I gave him herbs to smell. He smiled wanly. While he didn't have the strength to help make a bouquet as we had done the last time, he agreed that I could make one for him to put on his windowsill. He thanked me for my visit. I wished him well.

"Did you hear that Yitzhak died?" Thus a colleague greeted me when I arrived one morning at the rehab center. I was shaken but not surprised. I had last seen Yitzhak the week before when I visited him in his room, hoping to make a small bouquet with him or at least make one for him that I could leave next to his bed. I found him deeply asleep, curled in his bed, his cheeks hollow and his face gray. I sensed the end was near. Poor Yitzhak. He was such a sweet soul.

After hearing the news of Yitzhak's passing, I went into the small greenhouse on the roof. The first thing that caught my eye was a pot with an orange tag bearing the name Yitzhak, a date, and the word "cotton." The two stalks in the pot stood tall and straight. They were topped with bright green leaves. Though I never said goodbye to him, I felt as if Yitzhak had left me a farewell gift. I took the plant home with me.

Chapter 9

I Don't Have Any Connection to Plants.

During my internship at the rehab hospital, I had the opportunity to observe therapy sessions in the garden with a group of patients suffering from complex regional pain syndrome (CRPS). Also known as RSD (reflex sympathetic dystrophy), CRPS is a disorder that can occur in people of all ages. It manifests as severe chronic pain, usually in a leg or an arm. While the precise causal mechanisms are unknown, CRPS most often begins after an injury to or surgery on the affected limb. However, the pain is disproportionate to the original injury and may spread to other areas of the body. It may result in swelling of joints and a decreased ability to move the affected appendage. For many CRPS patients, the pain is so severe that they can no longer work or live independently. Not surprisingly, this often leads to depression.

The rehab center runs an outpatient program for patients with CRPS. Gardening is one of the therapeutic modalities employed with this population. The patients entering the garden for the first group meeting I attended all appeared to be in their late twenties or early thirties. A mixture of men and women, they each limped toward the table supported by a single crutch. The CRPS group met weekly, with new patients joining the ongoing group and old ones leaving when their referrals for outpatient care expired. Consequently, each meeting began with introductions. The new patients introduced themselves and were asked to say a few words about their relationship with plants. The veteran patients likewise gave their names and a word or two about themselves.

Leaning heavily on a crutch, a slim young woman with dark hair in a loose ponytail, wearing frayed jeans and a black T-shirt, slowly worked her way to the table. She slumped into a chair. As soon as the other young people had occupied most of the eight chairs around the table, there began a discussion of how long the group should wait for any stragglers. The consensus was they should only wait five minutes after the appointed time before beginning their activities. The young woman, who apparently was new to the group, was asked to introduce herself. "My name is Adi," she said. "I'm married to Amit—for the time being." With a look of indifference, she added, "I have a dog, but I don't have any connection to plants."

One of the participants asked to make tea with herbs from the garden before the formal activities began. She had also brought a snack for the group. Einat, the therapist leading the group, preferred to do the activity first and then have tea. At this point, I should note a universal aspect of Israeli culture. Every activity in Israel which involves more than one person must include a beverage and a snack. Whether a business meeting, a class, or a therapy session, people cannot sit down together without food and drink between them. The expression for the food or snacks served in such settings is *kibud*, which literally means

85

"honor." You honor your guests (or colleagues) by offering them something to eat and drink. Of course, the sessions I ran on the complex medical unit did not include food or beverages, as most of these patients either could not take food orally, were unable to feed themselves, or required a special diet.

Somehow, the subject of conversation turned to ginger. An animated discussion ensued concerning how to grow it and what it can be used for. "It's great in tea," someone pointed out. Another added, "You can't make Indian food without it." Adi just stared into her lap. The group moved on to talking about the potatoes they had planted a few weeks ago, while they set to work weeding a large pot in which they had planted cuttings. The final activity for that day was planting basil seeds. Each participant, except Adi, prepared individual pots, and together they mixed soil and compost, which they used to fill a large collective pot for the group.

Einat encouraged the participants to stand up while they worked to help strengthen their legs. They were also asked to fetch the soil, fill the watering cans, and otherwise be as active as possible. With these patients, gardening therapy serves multiple purposes. This group is part psychotherapy, part occupational therapy, and part physical therapy. The patients often become so involved in the task at hand—planting, weeding, watering—that they momentarily forget or at least overcome the pain that generally limits their activity and find themselves doing things they ordinarily would say they are incapable of doing. Patients who walk slowly into the garden dependent on a crutch to support them will often get up from the table without their crutch to find a spade or a pot. The therapist decided to hold future sessions around a higher table so that the participants would have to stand to work.

Further, Einat announced that, going forward, each week someone in the group would be assigned the task of presenting "the plant of the week." That person would be expected to do a bit of research into his or her chosen plant and come prepared to present their findings. Milia volunteered to make the presentation

on marijuana. This was not a surprising choice. Many patients suffering from CRPS find that marijuana (medical or otherwise) relieves their pain.

The following meeting began by going around the table asking people if they had any opening comments. Adi reported sadly that a cat had scratched her puppy, whom she referred to as *hakatana sheli* (my little one). The others shook their heads in sympathy. The group then looked at the progress of the tomato seeds they had planted two weeks earlier and the basil seeds they planted the week before. Most were excited to see that the flowerpots were jammed full of tiny sprouts. Adi showed no interest in the new growth in the pots.

Einat suggested that the sprouts would need to be thinned out to give plants room to spread their roots. This caused a dilemma for some of the patients. Thinning the sprouts means selecting which of these nascent plants will live and which will die. "How can we kill the seedlings we just planted?" "But if you do not uproot some of the plants, none will survive for lack of space." The simple act of thinning newly planted crops, which raises issues of attachment and the ability to let go, is rich in therapeutic potential.

Everyone except Adi reacted with awe when Einat brought over the pots of sunflowers which had grown from seeds planted a few weeks previously. This sparked a discussion of sunflower seeds and their benefits. Adi asked why the chili pepper seeds she planted hadn't sprouted. No one seemed to pay attention to her question. The group marveled at the progress of the potatoes, onions, and celery they had planted, adding soil to the potatoes and trimming the tops of the onions. They noted with pleasure that the mint cuttings had rooted after only three days. Someone explained that mint sends out runners, which grow into new plants and can take over a planter or a garden. At this point, everyone except Adi got up to fill small containers with soil in which to plant the sprigs of mint. "I'm depressed, but I don't want to talk about it," she said. And then added, "Everything is black." Milia complained of pain in her lower back and said she could not bend. The other members of the group stood as they carefully planted mint cuttings in small pots.

Once all the members have completed their planting, the custom is to close the group session by going around the table again, affording everyone a chance to make a concluding remark. Milia said, "It was really fun, a whole new world, creativity, therapy, and activity."

"It was very nice," commented Hadar, adding, "I had no connection to this before."

Milia remarked that she "learned not to be afraid."

Hadar chimed in, "I'm learning to love."

And then Adi spoke up. "It was marvelous. A unicorn!"

Listening to this, I was overwhelmed. How is it possible that just a few hours working in the garden could elicit such enthusiastic responses from previously disheartened and dejected patients? But I saw it with my own eyes. Plants are powerful.

Einat told the group that the following week they would be working with flowers. "I'd prefer to grow useful things," Adi responded, "not flowers."

"What's productive for you may not be productive for someone else," retorted Milia.

"We can do something productive, too," Einat interjected. "We'll transplant the basil."

Over the ensuing weeks, I watched as Adi started to enter the garden more briskly, though still with her crutch, and sit up straighter in her chair. She contributed more to group discussions. Adi explained that before she was stricken with CRPS, she worked in an office, and she and her husband had their own apartment. Because of her chronic severe pain, she had to stop working. This meant that she and her husband could no longer afford their apartment. They moved in with Adi's parents. She wasn't sure how long her marriage could survive under these circumstances.

Eventually, Adi also began participating more actively in the gardening tasks. She asked what kinds of plants do well

89

in sun versus shade. She wanted to know if she could plant basil cuttings and take them home to put in a window box in her apartment. "Perhaps I'll plant some other herbs, as well," she ventured.

Several weeks later, Hagit joined the group. She introduced herself saying, "I used to have a garden with my husband and children. But I can no longer plant. I can only pick from the garden now." "I like vegetables, but I have a problem with flowers," she explained. "Since my mother died, and they put flowers on her grave, flowers no longer do it for me. I associate flowers with death." Though she had said she was no longer able to work in the garden, by the end of her first session, Hagit asked to take home the celery she had planted. She said she wanted to "do something on my own in my garden at home." And she added that she wanted to learn to grow geraniums!

Gardening therapy, like any therapy, requires the therapist to be flexible and to be able to meet patients where they are. A patient who doesn't like flowers doesn't have to work with flowers. If they prefer "useful" plants, they can work with vegetables or herbs. If they don't like to get their hands dirty, they can wear gloves. Gardening therapy certainly does not work for all patients, but I have seen that many who initially respond with indifference or even hostility to plants, flowers, or gardening come to enjoy them and find them satisfying and therapeutic.

Chapter 10

At the Zoo

On my first day working in the complex medical unit, Orit, one of the veteran gardening therapists, introduced me to Ruchama. She sat in her wheelchair at the table in the center of the common room, where we held the gardening therapy "group," stringing beads. Ruchama did not seem at all pleased that Orit was handing the reins of the group to me, a stranger. She put her finger over the opening of her trach tube and, in a hoarse but quiet voice, said, "Why aren't you going to be here, Orit?" Orit explained that I was taking over the group on the unit. Ruchama scowled. Thereafter, for almost a year, each week when I greeted Ruchama, she replied, "Where's Orit? When is she coming?" I don't think Ruchama ever learned my name. She always addressed me as "Hey, you."

She was a small woman, perhaps in her late 60s. Her dark, chin-length hair, with prominent white roots, looked as if she'd slept on it. Her teeth were stained brown. Her wide-set dark eyes were surmounted by bushy eyebrows, and the random hair grew from her chin. Ruchama wore a tattered, hand-knit sweater over her hospital pajamas.

Ruchama began each session by saying she wasn't interested in planting or weeding or doing whatever activity I proposed. She preferred to continue reading the newspaper, stringing beads, or coloring. But after a few minutes, she would ask me to give her pots and soil and the other materials we were using that day. She especially loved to fill pots with soil, and did so very fast, using a tablespoon, rather than a spade. Some days, she didn't plant at all, but just filled pots. Once she filled twenty pots which she gave to another patient to use. At other times, after her initial resistance, she plunged enthusiastically into the day's project. She planted seeds and bulbs and was always eager to see their progress from week to week.

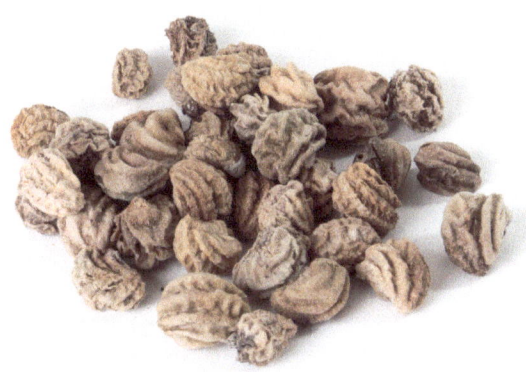

Ruchama didn't mind getting her hands dirty and used her fingers to push the seeds into the soil. She was very focused on planting the bulbs point up, as I had instructed her. She asked to see her scallion bulbs every week and marveled at their growth.

She also planted cilantro and basil. She thinned the seedlings and repotted them as they outgrew their tiny pots. And she planted nasturtium seeds. The Hebrew name for nasturtium is *covah hanazir*, which means "monk's hat," which should not be confused with the plant known in English as "monk's hood" (also known as aconitum, aconite, or wolf's bane), which has poisonous deep blue flowers. The nasturtium has edible orange, red, or yellow flowers in the shape of a pointed hat, hence the

name. In Israel, nasturtiums flower from early spring through mid to late summer (March through July or August). After the plant's brilliant blossoms have wilted, large seeds can easily be gathered from the seed pods which appear in their place.

The rehab center serves an ethnically mixed population, representative of the ethnic mix of Israel. There are Jews, religious and secular, Muslim Arabs, and Christians. There are Palestinians from the West Bank and Gaza. The patient population also includes foreign workers—Filipinos, Thai, Indian, etc. Likewise, the staff is a mix of Jews, Arabs, and Eritreans. Many of the staff are immigrants from the former Soviet Union. One hears Hebrew, Arabic, and Russian (as well as a smattering of other languages) spoken by the staff, the patients, and their families. Despite the diversity of the patients and the staff, the Jewish holidays are always acknowledged by the institution. Many of the units are decorated for the holidays, and activities are tailored to include traditional holiday symbols and customs.

Shavuot is a Jewish holiday in the late spring, falling seven weeks after Passover. It was originally a harvest festival, but it has also become a celebration of the giving of the Torah (the five books of Moses) at Mt. Sinai. It is customary, especially in Israel, to decorate the synagogues with freshly cut flowers. Schoolchildren often wear floral garlands. In honor of the holiday, I brought to the unit a bouquet of gazanias, a daisy-like flower that grows in a variety of rich colors—yellow, orange, bright pink, and purple—that I'd cut in the roof garden.

Ruchama presented an abrasive facade, and it took time for me to discover the caring, loving, even playful soul inside. I asked Ruchama if she would like me to make her a garland. She was tickled. I wove the stems together and put the flower crown on her head. She asked me to take a picture of her wearing the orange, yellow, and pink tiara and smiled and laughed giddily when I showed her the photograph.

On a few occasions, I brought raw peanuts in their shells for the group participants to plant in small pots. One need not even remove the nuts from the shells. Ruchama busied herself filling pots with soil and then pressed a whole peanut into the center of each pot. Ruchama turned to me holding a peanut in her hand and said, "When I was a kid, my father had a concession stand at the zoo in Tel Aviv."

"Wow, that's cool," I replied.

"He sold small paper bags of peanuts for people to feed to the animals," she continued. "I used to help him by filling the bags with peanuts," she recounted with pride and a dreamy look in her shiny brown eyes.

I took the pots with the peanuts up to the greenhouse. Two weeks later, they had sprouted, so I brought them back down to be transplanted into larger pots. Ruchama could barely contain her excitement at seeing the light green shoots emerging from the split peanut shells, which were still visible in the pots. With eagerness and determination, she gently removed the tiny seed-

lings and carefully transferred them to larger pots she had filled with soil. Again, she told me the story of her father's stand at the zoo and how she filled the bags with peanuts for him.

Ruchama suffers from diabetes with many complications, which necessitated her having a tracheostomy. For a long time, she was unable to walk, but after years of physical therapy, she learned to ambulate again. She is married and has two adult children, a son and a daughter, both of whom have developmental difficulties. They are both married and have their own children. Eventually, Ruchama warmed to me enough to tell me about her grandchildren's birthdays, and proudly announce the birth of a new grandchild. I knew that Ruchama had been at the rehab a long time. The staff told me that she ran her household remotely during the week and went home every weekend to cook and spend the Sabbath with her family. Occasionally, her husband would pick her up at the rehab and take her shopping at the shuk (the outdoor market) and bring her back.

At one point, Ruchama told me she would be discharged the following week. I was happy for her. But the following week, she was still there on the unit, telling me she would be leaving the next week. After several weeks of this, I started to wonder whether she would really be discharged soon, or whether that was just her hope. At long last, after over ten years as a patient there, Ruchama was indeed discharged from the rehab center. She excitedly went to live at home with her husband.

Chapter 11

They Who Sow in Tears Shall Reap with Songs of Joy

Early one morning, I received a message from the occupational therapist on the complex medical unit, suggesting I work with Rena, a new patient on the floor. Entering the common room with my cart loaded with pansies newly purchased from the nursery, I noticed a patient I hadn't seen on previous visits to the unit. She was seated in her wheelchair, with an oxygen tank attached, cannula in her nostrils. She faced a table at the side of the room, drinking a cup of tea. I approached her and asked her if her name was Rena. She looked up and smiled at me. "Yes," she said. "I'm Anne," I introduced myself. "I am a gardening therapist." Rena then glanced at the rainbow of flowers on my cart. "They are beautiful," she whispered, her Hebrew seasoned with a strong North African accent. Rena wore a gray knit hat, which covered most of her thick white hair. She was neatly dressed, a green knit top covered her ample bosom, and an aubergine shawl was draped over her shoulders.

"Would you like to plant flowers today?" Rena looked up at me, her brown eyes sparkling, and said, "With pleasure." I helped her put on an apron and covered the table with a plastic tablecloth (actually, a plastic trash bag I'd appropriated for this purpose). Removing a container of soil, a spade, and small terracotta-colored plastic pots from my cart, I explained to Rena that the small pansy plants needed to be transplanted from the trays in which they had come from the nursery into larger pots. She surveyed the supplies spread in front of her on the table and asked me to bring her rubber gloves so she wouldn't get her hands dirty. I found a pair of disposable gloves and stretched them over her hands, helping her insert her chubby fingers into the fingers of each glove.

The Hebrew name for pansy is *Amnon v' Tamar*, meaning Amnon and Tamar, the names of the characters in the Biblical story in Samuel II, chapter 13. Amnon and Tamar were half-brother and sister, children of King David. Amnon was infatuated with Tamar. He feigned illness so that she would come to his quarters to care for him. Then he raped her. Now, what does that have to do with a pansy?

There is a Russian folktale about Ivan and Maria, an elderly man and woman who each lived alone. They found one another and wed to relieve their loneliness. After they married, they began talking about their past and discovered that they were brother and sister. This realization tormented them, but God saved them by turning them into a single three-colored flower, which in Russian is called "Ivan and Maria."

Saul Tchernichovsky (1875–1943), the famous Russian-born Hebrew poet, translated the story of Ivan and Maria into Hebrew. In his version of the story, the protagonists are named Amnon and Tamar. And thus, the pansy is known by that name. However, the story isn't quite that simple. While the Hebrew language goes back thousands of years and has continued to be in active use for religious texts since that time, it was only in the 19th century that Hebrew was revived as the vernacular. In 1890, as the Jewish population of the future State of Israel began to grow and Hebrew was chosen as its official language, a Committee of the Hebrew Language was created to introduce new words into the language. That committee looked to the French word for the tri-color flower, *pensée*. Pensée means "thought," so the committee chose *machshava*, which is the Hebrew word for thought, as the name of the flower. But that name never caught on. In the 1930s, the committee created a subcommittee tasked with assigning names to plants and flowers. They chose the name *Amon v' Tamar* as the official name for the pansy. And it stuck.

I started to show Rena how to gently remove the small flowering plant from its tiny pot on the tray. She waved me aside. "I know what to do." Rena scooped soil from the container into the pots. After filling several pots with soil, she cautiously removed the small plants, one at a time, and placed each one in a hole in the soil she had made with her finger in the center of each pot. She patted down the soil around the transplanted plant. I complimented her on the efficiency with which she worked.

She asked if I had more plants for her to transplant. I looked at my cart and found succulent cuttings, which I put on the table in front of her. She looked at them and shook her head. "Don't you have any more flowers?" she asked me. I said that's all I had with me today, but that next time I would be sure to bring her more flowers to work with. With a bit less enthusiasm than before, Rena filled more pots with soil and planted the succulent cuttings. I suggested that she should water the plants in their new pots. "I don't think I can lift the watering can," she replied. "Don't worry," I reassured her, "I'll help you hold it." Together, we watered all the plants.

I lifted the apron over her head, and she held out her hands for me to remove her gloves. Then, as I placed the repotted plants on my cart and returned the other supplies and equipment, Rena reminded me, "Next time, be sure to bring plenty of flowers."

In addition to bringing Rena cuttings to root or plants to transplant, I occasionally brought her cut flowers she could

arrange into small bouquets by inserting the stems into a floral sponge at the bottom of a cup. Rena made artful flower arrangements. She often asked me to bring one of her arrangements to her bedridden roommate or to the nurses, many of them young Arab men, at the desk in the unit. They always responded with enthusiasm when I told them the flowers were from Rena, and I relayed their gratitude back to her. She smiled contentedly.

At other times, Rena kept the bouquets for herself and would show me the previous week's arrangement on the windowsill next to the table where she sat. She explained that she had conscientiously watered them all week. When there were coleus cuttings among the cut flowers, she pointed out with satisfaction that they had grown roots since the week before and could be planted.

Rena derived such joy from her windowsill garden. Unfortunately, COVID again reared its head in the unit. One of the patients tested positive and was removed to a nursing facility. The entire unit was placed in quarantine. This meant the patients were yet again confined to their rooms and did not have any of the activities that normally brought relief to the boredom of life in the complex nursing unit. Therapists like me were not allowed to enter the unit. For a patient as active and sociable as Rena, this was particularly difficult. I learned from the staff of the unit that Rena fell into a depression and spent a lot of time crying while confined to her room.

When the period of quarantine ended, Rena was relieved to be able to go again to the common room, do crafts, play games, and enjoy the company of others. However, her spirits fell when she saw that, in her absence, no one had watered her plants and arrangements in the windowsill. The herbs she lovingly planted and used for her tea were wilted and the cut flowers had died.

I met Rena that day with a particularly large and colorful bunch of cut flowers—many varieties of geraniums, snapdragons, lantana, and others. "Would you like to arrange flowers, Rena?" I asked, certain of her response.

"Yes," she replied enthusiastically, "but first," she said, with a sad look in her eyes, "look at my ruta plant." Indeed, the leaves were shriveled and drooping, and the thin stem looked brittle.

"Rena, the leaves are still green," I observed. "Maybe we can salvage it by watering it." I brought her a watering can, and she watered it well. I returned the pot to the windowsill, and we crossed our fingers.

Ruta (or ruda) is a Middle Eastern herb, sometimes used in tea. It is also one of the fragrant plants that can be used for the blessing of spices during the Havdala ceremony at the end of the Jewish Sabbath. There are those who attribute spiritual

properties to ruta. Asnat, one of Rena's roommates, a young woman with developmental delays in addition to a host of medical issues, urgently demanded that I bring her a ruta plant from the garden to keep next to her bed. She explained that the plant is a charm and will bring her good fortune. The following week, I brought Asnat a small ruta plant. She was thrilled. I don't know if the plant has had any salutary effects on Asnat's condition but having it beside her bed makes her feel protected.

Having addressed the ruta problem, Rena applied herself with extra zeal to the task of arranging flowers, grinning radiantly as she surveyed the results. She worked so fast and determinedly that part way through the session I had to go back to the garden to cut more flowers. As she selected and trimmed the flowers for each bouquet, she told me how difficult it had been for her to be confined to her room and how much the plants and flowers she works with and saves on the windowsill contribute to her life. She also told me about a friend and fellow patient with COVID who was no longer in the unit and unlikely to return. At the end of our session, I asked Rena if I could take a picture of her with the magnificent bouquets she'd created. She was delighted and smiled broadly for the photo, which I sent to her on WhatsApp so she could share it with her family. I showed the photo to other members of the staff, who were amazed and delighted to see Rena smiling again.

One day, when I came to the unit, a handsome man who looked to be in his early 50s was talking animatedly with Rena. She introduced me to her son Yossi. I chatted briefly with him, and he told me how much his mother loved plants, especially flowers. "I have seen that," I told him. I suggested that perhaps now that the weather was a bit cooler, his mother might like to come up to the roof garden for individual sessions with me there. That appealed both to Yossi and to Rena. I later learned from Rena that Yossi was one of her four children. With tears in her eyes, Rena told me that her daughter had died eight years ago, leaving six orphaned children.

For this session, I brought Rena "baby" spider plants, which already had tiny roots and were ready to be planted in soil. Rena filled twelve small pots with soil and deftly planted all the baby plants. We agreed that the following week we would meet in the garden.

At the appointed hour, a young volunteer wheeled Rena up to the roof garden. In addition to its staff, the rehab center relies heavily on an army of volunteers, most of whom are deployed transporting wheelchair-bound patients from their rooms to their various therapy sessions and back. Many of these volunteers are young Germans who come to Israel for a couple of years to fulfill their German national-service requirement. There are also volunteers from Scandinavian countries and the occasional American. The hospital provides the volunteers with on-campus housing, cafeteria meals, and a small allowance. The lingua franca among the volunteers and between the volunteers and the staff is English, though some of the veteran volunteers have picked up sufficient Hebrew to understand simple instructions and to have some basic communication with patients.

One of the German volunteers is an older woman who, after her retirement, began coming to Israel for four to six months a year to volunteer at the hospital. Although, like most of the volunteers, she is not Jewish, she met other German speakers in Israel, who introduced her to the Yiddish cultural center in Tel Aviv. There, she picked up some Yiddish, a language that derives from Hebrew and medieval German. She has found that knowing Yiddish facilitates her communication with some of the older Russian-speaking patients, who speak neither Hebrew nor English, but who learned Yiddish in childhood.

I greeted Rena when she arrived on the roof and wheeled her to the table where I had gathered the materials for our session. Rena immediately asked to see the spider plants she had planted the previous week. They were already on the table waiting for her. She saw that they had grown and were ready to be transplanted to larger pots. Rena applied herself to the task with energy and enthusiasm. At one point, she asked me to bring her a glass of water. I fetched the water, handed her the glass, and listened as she quietly intoned the Hebrew blessing before taking a sip.

While she worked, she told me a bit about her background. Rena is 86 years old but appears younger. She came to Israel from Morocco with her family 70 years ago. The family—eight boys and Rena, the middle child and only girl—lived in *ma'abarot,* transit camps that in the 1950s housed new immigrants in tents and shacks until more permanent dwellings were available. They eventually moved to a development town in the South of Israel. Rena later lived on a *moshav* (a cooperative agricultural community) in the desert. She married, had her children, divorced, moved to another moshav, remarried, and divorced again. She was employed working in the kitchen of a preschool. She now

lives in Yafo. Rena told me proudly that while she was living on the moshav, she grew lots of plants in pots in front of her house.

After Rena had finished repotting the spider plants, I took her on a tour of the garden in her wheelchair. In my initial encounters with Rena, she preferred working with flowers, but when she worked in the garden, she was particularly taken with the eggplants, hot peppers, and kohlrabi. The cotton plant, festooned with fluffy wads of ripe cotton, she told me wistfully, reminded her of picking cotton on the moshav in her youth. In the herb corner, I cut samples of mint, rosemary, *sheba*, basil, thyme, and other herbs for her to smell. Even with the oxygen cannula in her nostrils, she was able to inhale deeply and take in the familiar fragrances. "May I take some back with me for my tea?" she asked.

"Of course," I replied. I gave her generous sprigs of mint, melissa, and lemon geranium to bring back to the unit. She cheerfully agreed to continue meeting weekly in the garden, weather permitting.

One Tuesday, just before my scheduled session with Rena in the garden, I received the following message from the Finnish volunteer who had gone to fetch Rena from the unit: "She doesn't want to come. She has paint *[sic]* in her hand." Bewildered, I reread the message. Thinking perhaps Rena was preoccupied with a painting project, I replied to the volunteer that I would go down to the unit to see Rena. When I got there, Rena complained to me that she wouldn't be able to do any gardening today as she had *pain in her hand*. I suggested that I wheel her up to the garden anyway, where she could at least enjoy the sunshine, fresh air, and a change of scenery. She agreed. Once we got to the roof, I wheeled Rena to the table where I had laid out the plants and soil I had planned for her to work with. Her task was to repot flowers from small pots into a single large flower box. She shook her head despairingly and repeated that her hands hurt. "No problem," I said. "You can tell me what to do, and I will be your hands." Thus we began, with her instructing me on what to do,

109

and my following her instructions. But, before long, Rena reached out and took the spade from my hand to dig a hole in the flower box. She grabbed a small pot and, using both her hands, gently removed the plant and repotted it in the larger planter. And so it continued.

As I have often seen, people who protest that they can't do a particular activity will begin to do it once they see tangible results. Or, perhaps it's a variation of the Tom Sawyer whitewashing the fence phenomenon. Regardless of what motivates the patient to undertake an action they thought they were unable to do, its therapeutic effect is enormous.

One morning I showed Rena the cherry tomatoes I had brought to the hospital and asked her if she wanted to plant them. "Yes!" she replied. I explained to her that we could just cut the tomatoes in half and plant half a tomato in each of the seedling pots. Rena enthusiastically and meticulously filled the pots, six per tray, with soil. With her index finger, she gently dug a hole in the center of each small pot and carefully placed the half tomato inside. She sprinkled more soil to cover the tomato. As she did so, almost under her breath, I could hear her recite in Hebrew the passage from Psalms 126:5: "They who sow in tears shall reap with songs of joy."

I told Rena I would put the pot in the greenhouse. "It will take a couple of weeks for the seeds to sprout, right?"

"Yes, we should see some sprouts in about two weeks," I confirmed. "At least, I hope so." As I wrote out tags to place in the pots ("Rena, unit 13, cherry tomatoes"), I said the date, "January 2" aloud. Rena smiled broadly and exclaimed, "Today's my birthday!"

"*Mazal tov!* (Congratulations!)," I said. "Wishing you good health until 120!"

She beamed. Then she said, "You are the first to wish me a happy birthday. My children haven't called me yet today." As we parted, I waved and again wished her a happy birthday. She responded with a huge grin.

Chapter 12

Bridging a Cultural Divide

"Anne, could you help me?" Einat, one of the gardening therapists, called out to me with desperation in her voice. "Orit is out today, and I have a large outpatient group-therapy session now. I need someone to work with Ahmed."

"I'm expecting a patient to arrive in the garden for individual therapy in a few minutes," I replied, "but I'd be happy to work with Ahmed until my patient arrives."

I saw him sitting on a chair next to a table in the garden, a young man with olive skin, dark eyes, closely cropped black hair, and a bit of a goatee. He wore black pants, a black T-shirt with an English slogan, and black athletic shoes. He was shorter than average, with a sturdy, muscular upper body. His crutches were propped against a flower bed.

As she left to go back to her group, Einat said something to me about bringing Ahmed the pots of figs he had planted so he could add compost to them and pointed vaguely in the direction of one of the garden shelves. I introduced myself to Ahmed and asked him where his figs were. He pointed to several large pots and a window box containing bright green, healthy-looking young fig trees. I brought him the window box and a container of compost. He asked what the compost was. I explained that it was organic fertilizer that would enrich the soil. He deftly added small quantities of compost to the pots and carefully mixed it into the soil. I apologized that I couldn't stay very long with him as I had a patient coming shortly. With his head down, staring into his lap, he said it didn't matter. "I am just fed up. I've had it with all this treatment. I don't feel like doing anything." I told him it was OK for him just to sit in the garden if he wanted to.

Ahmed sat for a few minutes. At this point, it was apparent that my patient was not coming for his session. I returned to Ahmed. "It seems my patient is not coming. Would you like to do some more planting?" "Ok, why not," was his less than enthusiastic reply. I brought him some tiny herb and geranium plants that had been rooted by patients who had since been discharged. The plants were ready to be transplanted to larger pots. Ahmed recognized the za'atar plant and was eager to transplant it. I also showed him basil (*reyhan* in Arabic) and a type of mint (*nana* in both Arabic and Hebrew), which he was not familiar with. Without much instruction, he arranged empty

113

pots, filled them with soil to which he added compost, and gently removed the herbs from their tiny pots. He examined the roots in the ball of soil that he extracted from each small pot. On a couple of occasions, he noticed that the roots were infested with ants and pointed out to me the ant eggs in the soil. "We better get rid of these," he correctly advised. I complimented him on his vigilance and knowledge of gardening.

When he finished transplanting the first tray of herbs I had given him, I asked if he wanted to continue. "Yes," he said enthusiastically.

As he worked, we talked. "You certainly seem to know what to do with plants," I observed. "Do you have experience gardening?"

"I used to have a garden," Ahmed replied. "I grew all kinds of herbs and vegetables. But I don't anymore."

Ahmed lives in one of the larger mixed Arab-Jewish towns in Israel and comes to the rehab center as an outpatient in their "day hospitalization" program. He used to work very hard, driving a truck sometimes 24 hours a day ("You have no idea how tiring that is."). He also worked in a scrap metal business. Now, since his injury, he just sits around the house, he told me, lowering his eyes and shaking his head. His pain is so bad, he can't work.

Our conversation turned back to herbs. He told me that he loves to cook with herbs and that every dish he makes calls for different ones. Most of all, he likes to prepare meat. I asked if he grills the meat or cooks it on the stove. Ahmed said he does both but prefers dishes cooked on the stove. Sometimes, he will grill the meat, then put it in a pot to cook with liquid, herbs, and vegetables. One of his favorite recipes involves cooking meat in Coca-Cola."

"Coca-Cola?" I repeated, not certain I'd understood him.

"Yes, it tenderizes the meat and gives it flavor."

Another recipe he described involves cooking meat in *leben* (a dairy product much like yogurt). Ahmed paused and looked up at me, "You don't cook meat in milk, do you?" he asked, referring to the Biblical prohibition of cooking a kid in its mother's milk, which is the source of the kashrut laws that observant Jews follow.

"You're right," I nodded, smiling, "I don't cook meat with milk."

Ahmed said that another of his culinary "tricks" is to soak the meat in water before cooking it. That gets all the blood out. He explained that cooking meat with blood results in a scum on the surface of the cooking liquid. It's cleaner, and the results are better if you remove the blood first. "You know, kosher meat is also soaked to remove the blood before cooking," I told him. We both smiled.

After he had transplanted and watered a dozen small plants, he looked again at the *nana* plant. "We have all kinds of mint," he said, "but I've never seen this variety. Would it be OK for me to take it home?"

"Certainly, you can take as many of these plants as you like."

"Could you put it in a bag for me? With my crutches, I can't carry it without a bag."

"No problem." I brought him a bag and put the mint plant inside.

After a lull in our conversation, Ahmed told me that the only thing he plants now are succulents. They are so easy to grow and need so little care. They thrive without much water and will root anywhere. We talked about the huge variety of succulents and how interesting the different shapes and textures are. "Just a minute," I said. "I have a wonderful book about succulents. Let me show you." I ran inside and brought back a beautifully illustrated book. "It's in English, but I think you'd enjoy looking at the photos." I handed him the book. As he turned the pages, he pointed to various plants: "I have one like this... I used to have one of these with the white spines... I really like this one..." We talked about how well these plants have adapted to adverse conditions. I thought, if I continue working with Ahmed, we must do a session or two with succulents.

When the time came to end our session, Ahmed started to push himself up from the chair where he'd been seated for
an hour. Wincing with pain, he pushed down on the arms of the
chair and tried to straighten his legs. His left leg buckled under

him. He reached for his crutches and, grimacing, managed to get his body upright. I handed him the plastic bag with his mint plant. He took it and tried to adjust his hand to hold the crutch and the bag at the same time. "No, I don't think this will work," he said with frustration. "Please keep this for me. I'll take it home another time—with the figs."

As he hobbled off, Einat approached me. Out of the corner of her eye she had observed some of my sessions with Ahmed and was amazed. "What a transformation!" She told me that Ahmed had been in her outpatient group, but his overflowing anger was disruptive. He talked about how the doctors had misled him about the results of his surgery and how he wanted to take vengeance on them. He complained constantly of his pain and inability to support his family. Ahmed has two young children, she told me. He had told the group that his son asked him for 5 shekels ($1.25) to buy something. "I used to earn a good living, now I can't even afford to give my son 5 shekels." He felt emasculated.

During my brief encounter with him, Ahmed expressed frustration and sadness but none of the intense anger which he had voiced in the group sessions. In fact, while he was working with the plants, he seemed transported from his current physical reality with its pain and limitations.

The interaction between Ahmed, an Israeli Arab, and me, an Israeli Jew, is hardly exceptional. Israel's healthcare system is perhaps the most dramatic example of the natural integration of Israeli Jews and Arabs. In the waiting rooms of every hospital and clinic, one sees Arab women in hijabs sitting next to haredi men with *payot* (sidecurls) and big black hats alongside young women in tank tops and shorts. The staff of medical facilities—not only in mixed cities like Jerusalem, Haifa, and Ramla but in Tel Aviv, too—include a patchwork of religious and secular Jews, Muslim and Christian Arabs, and others. About 70 percent of the pharmacists at the largest Israeli drugstore chain, SuperPharm, are Arabs, who make up a similarly high proportion of the physical therapists

118

and nurses one encounters. Of course, the families comforting and consoling one another in the ICU and ventilator units are from every possible walk of life; differences in faith, dress, and culture all but evaporate in settings of suffering and loss.

Every year, the rehab hospital organizes a carnival to celebrate the Jewish holiday of Purim. Purim is a festive holiday commemorating the story in the Book of Esther about the salvation of the Jews of ancient Persia from a decree commanding their annihilation. It is customary to have parties and dress in costumes. The rehab hospital's carnival is for the amusement of children who are patients there and the children of hospital staff. One of the young patients, confined to a wheelchair, was being pushed from booth to booth by a Muslim therapist on staff who wore bunny ears over her hijab and a cotton tail pinned to her tunic. Another disabled child was accompanied by an Eritrean staff member, a gold cross hanging prominently from a chain around her neck. In the corner of the hospital courtyard, a man played an accordion and sang, in Hebrew, the Purim classic: "Oh today we'll merry, merry be, and nash some hamentashen."

Chapter 13

Thumbs Up

At first, it was almost hard to look at her, helplessly slumped
to one side in her wheelchair. A tracheostomy tube with mucus
oozing from it protruded from her throat. One hand, curled into
a permanent fist, rested on the tray attached to her chair. She had
a prominent overbite, which caused her mouth to remain slightly
open. Batsheva was always well groomed, her dark hair pulled
tightly back in a short ponytail, away from her thin, olive-com-
plected face. Her clothes were clean and tidy. She generally wore
a handknit sweater and, regardless of the season, draped a plaid
woven shawl over her narrow shoulders. It was difficult for me to
estimate her age, though I later learned she was in her mid-60s.
Often, when I entered the common area, Batsheva would be fast
asleep in her chair. But when she was awake, or when I'd awaken
her to join the gardening therapy group, her dark brown eyes
would open wide, and she'd greet me with a warm smile.

Batsheva was cognitively intact but physically very limited. She couldn't speak because of the trach tube, but she communicated with her eyes and gestures with her left hand. Except when she was so sleepy that she could not keep her eyes open, Batsheva was keen to participate in the gardening activities. I tailored a project specifically for her each week, since even her functioning hand had only a limited range of motion and very little strength. Occasionally, I had to persuade her to loosen her grip on the wad of tissues she clutched in her left hand to absorb the thick drool, which she couldn't control, so that she could take part in the activity. But, once her hand was free, it was clear she was ready and excited to get to work.

One of the activities Batsheva enjoyed was decorating potted succulents with small white stones. I placed a small pot with a succulent in front of her and gave her a shallow dish of small, smooth white stones. Batsheva carefully picked up a stone between her slender thumb and forefinger, slowly lifted her hand, and deposited the stone on the soil surrounding the plant in the pot. She worked meticulously, selecting stones one at a time and mindfully placing each one in the pot, until no soil was visible between the stones. Some days, she decorated 4 or 5 pots before she grew fatigued. On a good day, she had the strength to water the plants when she finished decorating them with stones.

One week, Batsheva planted dill. Using a tablespoon, she slowly and carefully lifted spoons full of soil from the container into small plastic pots. At times, when her energy flagged, I helped her lift her hand so that the soil would go into the pot. She then carefully picked up the seeds, sprinkled them on surface of the soil, and covered them with another spoonful of dirt. I helped her hold a small watering can with which to water the seeds. She was delighted when, a few weeks later, I brought her the pots with tender, green shoots poking their heads out from the soil. Over the course of the years, Batsheva planted nasturtium seeds, green onion bulbs, and transplanted petunias. Her face lit up each time I brought her the small plants that emerged from the seeds and bulbs she had planted.

Another favorite project was weeding flowerpots. I brought down from the garden large pots or flowerboxes with plants in the center and a profusion of small weeds crowding the soil around them. Batsheva carefully plucked out the tiny weeds, one at time, with her thumb and forefinger, making sure not to miss any. I was impressed with the enthusiasm she displayed while doing this task. On other occasions, Batsheva would clean up potted plants by plucking the dead leaves off the stems and removing any wilted flowers. She proceeded fastidiously and had no trouble identifying which leaves to pick. She took obvious pride in doing a thorough job. I congratulated her profusely, and she replied with a smile and an emphatic thumbs up with her left hand.

There were times she tired before she had finished the task, leaned her head to the side, and fell asleep. Sometimes, a coughing fit would interrupt her work with the plants, and she busied herself wiping off the mucus she coughed up. It was then difficult to persuade her to continue the project she had begun. But in general, Batsheva was anxious to complete any activity she started and showed her satisfaction with her trademark thumbs-up in my direction.

New therapists ask me how I determine which activities to pursue with a particular patient. Of course, the decision is primarily driven by the individual's therapeutic needs and goals. Since gardening therapy at this hospital falls under the umbrella of occupational therapy, I seek activities that involve the skill that needs to be developed. For some patients, we focus on small motor activities, such as using the fingers to pick up and manipulate small objects—seeds, for example, or pulling up small weeds. Others need to work on larger motor skills, which can be accomplished through filling pots with soil or lifting a watering can. However, for many of the more limited patients, the therapeutic value lies in an activity that has a goal or a purpose. With that objective in mind, the choice of the specific project is determined by the individual patient's abilities. Another factor influencing my choice of activities is the season. Most seeds should be planted and flower or bear fruit at specific times of the year. Planting seeds for summer flowers in the fall is a recipe for disappointment.

Batsheva is a good example. Our primary therapeutic goal was to encourage her to use her functioning hand as much as possible, to lift her hand, open her grip, and use her fingers to pick up and place objects deliberately. And, because the activities have a purpose—decorating the pot of succulents with small stones, removing dead leaves from a plant, or weeding a pot—the patient is more motivated than they would be simply doing an exercise, such as moving an object from one cup to another. Moreover, people derive satisfaction from seeing and touching the product of their labor. Batsheva, for example, was clearly delighted to see the flowers that grew from the seeds she herself had planted. For the most part, gardening therapy for the severely handicapped is often a matter of stimulating the senses—smelling herbs and fragrant flowers, looking at brightly colored blossoms—or the tactile stimulation of touching hard, soft, smooth, fuzzy, sharp, or fleshy plant material.

On occasion, Batsheva's husband, a small, quiet man wearing a knitted *kippah* (yarmulka), would wheel her into the common room for the gardening therapy session, then leave. I learned that Batsheva had been in the rehab center for 20 years (since she was in her mid 40s). She was the mother of four children, all of whom were supportive and visited frequently. Her husband was extremely devoted and, according to the staff, always by her side. He left his job as a driver at a transportation company a few years previously to be with her every day.

The discomfort I felt when I first encountered Batsheva turned to eager anticipation. I looked forward to working with her. With just a little encouragement, she could do so much. Her pride and pleasure in her accomplishments was contagious. Unfortunately, COVID-19 was also contagious. At the same time I contracted COVID, I later learned, so did Batsheva. And, in her case, with her greatly compromised health, it proved fatal. When I returned to work after I had recovered, I was devastated to learn that Batsheva had succumbed to the virus.

Chapter 14

Parsley, Sage, Rosemary & Thyme

As I walked through the courtyard of the rehab center, pushing my cart loaded with pots of bright green herbs, a woman stopped me. She was dressed smartly in black slacks, with a black sweater over a white blouse. Neatly coiffed chin-length brown hair framed her pleasant unmade-up round face. I had noticed her a few minutes earlier, holding her cell phone screen in front of the young man who sat motionless in the wheelchair beside her. He was bundled in blankets, with one covering his head like a hood. The olive skin on his cheeks looked smooth with only a hint of whiskers. He had thick black eyebrows over his soft brown eyes, his gaze fixed on something the woman seemed to be trying to show him.

The woman's wide, dark eyes looked at me beseechingly over her COVID face mask. In Hebrew, I asked the woman how I could help her. It quickly became apparent that she spoke no Hebrew. I tried again in English. She replied in broken English, deeply accented with Arabic, "Could I have herbs for my son to smell?"

"Certainly," I replied. I immediately gave her a few fragrant sprigs of basil, rosemary, and lavender. "I'm so sorry, but I must hurry to meet with patients in the next building. Otherwise, I'd be happy to stay to work with your son." I then asked what unit her son was on. It happened that he was in the complex medical unit, where I regularly see patients. "I work on that unit," I told her. "And I'd be happy to bring him herbs to smell next Tuesday when I'm there. What's his name?" I asked.

"Khalid," she replied.

"Good, I will go to see him next week."

Khalid, who was 35 years old but looked younger, had contracted COVID. After he recovered, he began suffering from severe headaches. Initially, this was thought to be a long-term effect of the virus. But a brain scan showed that he had an aneurysm. He was operated on, following which he fell into a coma for several months. Although he emerged from the coma, it was not clear to the medical staff how aware he was of his surroundings. He had not shown much response to stimuli.

The following week, I met Khalid and his mother in the unit. His eyes were no longer fixed but were moving left and right, seemingly scanning his field of vision. I brought cuttings from all the various herbs we had growing in the roof garden, hoping at least one of them would trigger a response from Khalid. One by one, I selected herbs and held them under his nose. First, I tried mint. When he blinked his eyes in an apparent response to the fragrance, his mother's wide, normally sad eyes met mine over our masks. We were both surprised and delighted. I tried again with rosemary, the same response. And then with za'atar and lavender.

Each time I picked out an herb, I said its name in English and gave it to Khalid's mother to sniff before giving it to him. I asked her what the plant was called in Arabic, repeated the name for Khalid, and promptly forgot it. (I have a hard time with names—of people and plants—regardless of the language.) However, I did remember the Arabic word for basil. In Hebrew, basil has two names, *bazilicom* and *rey'chan,* the latter derived from the Hebrew word for fragrance or smell, *reyach.* The Arabic word for basil, *rey'han,* is just a slightly different version of the second Hebrew name for the herb. Likewise, nana is the word for mint in both Hebrew and Arabic.

Khalid's mother suggested I touch the leaves to his nose. This provoked an even more dramatic response. He jerked his head back and blinked his eyes. I don't know whether this was simply a reflex or a conscious reaction to the stimulus. I tried more herbs under his nose. In most cases, he seemed to react by either blinking or closing his eyes. Then I stroked his cheek with a bunch of soft, "furry" sage leaves. There was no noticeable reaction. Finally, I held a bright red kalanchoe floret in front of his eyes and slowly moved it left and right. I may be engaging in wishful thinking, but it seemed he followed it, ever so slightly, with his eyes. I left Khalid's mother with the herb cuttings in a cup of water so that she could present them to him again later. His mother thanked me profusely, and we agreed to meet the following week after his physical therapy session.

Each time we met, Khalid's mother greeted me warmly. She pushed her son's wheelchair to a quiet corner of the common room on the unit, where she could sit next to him while I gave him herbs to smell. With time, Khalid's reactions to the smell of the herbs I held under his nose became more distinct. The *sheba*, za'atar, thyme, lavender, and rosemary, each in succession, prompted Khalid to close his eyes in a very deliberate way. As I presented each herb, I would say Khalid's name and the name of the herb. In the case of mint and lemon geranium, I also said, in English, that they are used for tea. I suggested we see what would happen if Khalid touched some of the leaves with his hands. His mother gently removed Khalid's left hand from under the blanket. A small pillow was strapped loosely inside his fist to prevent his hand from permanently curling shut. I selected a textured sage leaf and gently rubbed it against some of his fingertips. I didn't notice any reaction. I tried a more roughly textured leaf, and he closed his eyes in response. Progress?

As I presented herbs to Khalid, I conversed with his mother in English. "Are you here every day?"

"Yes."

"Where do you live?"

129

"In the West Bank." (I was aware that Palestinians from the "West Bank" are regularly among the patients at the hospital. In fact, a lovely Chinese orange tree in the roof garden was the gift of a Palestinian farmer in gratitude for the care he received there.)

"Wow," I responded. "How do you get here?"

"Either by bus or by private car, but sometimes I stay overnight at the hospital." Apparently, the Palestinian Authority pays for Khalid's mother to have a room where she can stay overnight at the hospital to avoid daily trips back and forth.

"Do you have other children, in addition to Khalid?" I wanted to know.

"Three children—a male [pointing to Khalid] and two female."

"Oh," I replied. "I also have three children, two sons and a daughter." I asked if her son was married.

"Yes, he is married."

"Does he have children?"

"A male and a female."

"How old are they?" I inquired.

"The male is five, and the female is three."

She then took out her phone and scrolled through Arabic WhatsApp messages to find photos of Khalid's children to show me—an adorable little boy with dark hair and dark eyes in a play car at a playground and a photo of the same boy being hugged by his little sister, who strongly resembled him.

"They are beautiful," I exclaimed. She nodded, glancing wistfully at her paralyzed son in his wheelchair.

Khalid's mother was the picture of quiet elegance and grace. Every time I saw her, she was dressed simply but smartly in tailored black slacks, leather shoes or boots with a dark sweater, and—in cooler weather—a plain black quilted coat. Though a small woman, she stood out from the other patients' family members because of her understated stylishness. She personally wheeled her son from therapy to therapy, rather than relying on

130

volunteers or staff members. She often seemed shy and reluctant to engage others in conversation, but that may be in part because she did not speak any Hebrew, though the institution has many Arab patients and a large complement of Arab nurses, therapists, aides, and other staff. In my first several meetings with her, I had the sense she felt isolated and lonely, with only her son, who was severely disabled, to speak to. That may in part explain her apparent pleasure at our meetings.

Lavender, rosemary, lemon geranium, and a certain variety of basil grow abundantly all over Israel. They require no cultivation. Once planted in an area with enough light and moisture, they flourish and spread. In many parts of Israel, one sees hedges of rosemary. Lemon geranium proliferates as a ground cover, lending its distinctive fragrance to the surroundings. Similarly, lavender and an intensely scented variety of basil with dark green or purple leaves grow wild and lushly. The grounds of the hospital are planted with many of these hardy herbal shrubs. I periodically go downstairs, shears in hand, to "harvest" herbs to use with my patients. On one such occasion, I was pleased to see Khalid's mother sitting on a bench in the courtyard chatting amiably with three other Arab women, each wearing a hijab and an ankle-length button-down coat. One of the women, a double amputee, was seated in a hospital wheelchair. When I walked over to greet Khalid's mother, the woman in the wheelchair noticed the herbs in my hand and asked if she could have a few branches to smell. "*Shokran* (thank you)," she said to me in Arabic when I gave her the cuttings. I asked Khalid's mother how to say "you're welcome," and responded to the woman with my best effort. The women laughed.

It is not unusual for both patients and staff who spot me walking in the rehab center carrying a jar of cut herbs or notice a bunch of fragrant cuttings on my cart to ask if they can have some. Sometimes they simply help themselves to a sprig or two to sniff while we ride together on the elevator. (I always tell them to keep them.) One day, the elevator was moving so slowly that I was able to conduct an impromptu gardening therapy session with a patient who happened to be in the car. Seated in his wheelchair, he was curious about the cuttings on my cart. I handed him one herb after another. He smelled each of them and tried to identify it. When the doors finally opened on his floor, he was reluctant to leave. Smiling warmly, he thanked me for making his day. I don't know whether sniffing herbs is more common in the Middle East than in North America, but I can't imagine people in the large hospital where I worked in Boston asking for herbs to smell.

At the close of the Jewish Sabbath (Saturday evening) each week, traditional Jews perform a ceremony called *Havdalah* ("separation"). This ritual marks the end of the day of rest and joy and the beginning of the regular work week. It has three parts—a blessing said over a cup of wine, a blessing on a multi-wicked candle (since during the Sabbath one is prohibited from lighting fires), and a blessing thanking God for creating fragrant herbs or spices, which are then sniffed as part of the ceremony. The most common explanation for including herbs or spices is to comfort the soul, which is saddened by the departure of the "extra soul" one received on the Sabbath. Many view this "extra soul" as a metaphor for the relaxation, joy, and celebration that are part of Sabbath observance. However, according to the Zohar, the foundational work of Jewish mystical thought, first published in thirteenth-century Spain but believed to have originated much earlier, the extra soul is not simply a state of mind but literally another soul that accompanies a person during the Sabbath. At the end of the Sabbath, the original soul mourns its loss and is consoled by the sweet fragrance of the spices.

But why would a pleasant scent be used to ease the soul's pain? Some say this goes back to the Garden of Eden. When Adam and Eve sinned by eating the fruit of the tree of knowledge, they used all their senses except the sense of smell. The verse (Genesis 3:6–8) states: "The woman *saw*... and she *took*... and he *ate*... they *heard*..." The sense of smell is not mentioned and apparently was not involved in this sin. As a result, smell is

considered the most refined of the five senses and the one most enjoyed by the soul.

Regardless of whether one accepts this interpretation, it is universally recognized that smells are evocative, and those that evoke pleasant memories and associations can have a salutary effect on one's spirit. One of the patients in the complex medical unit was an 88-year-old gentleman named Shmuel. In contrast to most of the patients on that unit, who were in wheelchairs if they could get out of bed at all, Shmuel used a walker. Whenever I was on the unit, I spied Shmuel's diminutive figure, a navy knit ski cap on his head, wandering through the halls or seated at the table in the common room. Also, unlike most of the patients on the unit, Shmuel usually had a sweet smile on his face. He told me that he had been an elementary school teacher many years

ago. I used to propose a gardening activity to him whenever I saw him. He consistently declined. "I have more important things to think about," he told me more than once, with a twinkle in his blue eyes. I eventually caught on and stopped asking.

Once, however, I noticed that Shmuel was not pushing his walker around the unit, nor was he seated with the morning paper in the common room. I found him in bed in his room. Clearly, he was not feeling well. I proposed making him a small bouquet of flowers. "No, thanks," he shook his head. "Would you like to smell some herbs?" I offered. A trace of a smile crossed his lips. "Yes, thank you," he whispered. I handed him a small cluster of assorted herb cuttings. He inhaled deeply and, with a big grin, said, "Herbs awaken the soul." I left the cuttings in a cup of water next to his bed and wished him well. The next time I saw him, he was up and about as before, wearing his trademark navy knit ski cap, an elfin glint in his eyes.

In Khalid's case, giving him herbs to sniff was less about reviving the soul, though it may have had that effect, than about stimulating his sensory nerves and trying to heal neural connections in his brain. Later in the day, after seeing his mother and her friends in the courtyard, I met Khalid and his mother in his room. He was lying on his back in bed, his arms at his side, covered by the blanket. His brown eyes were open, staring off to the side. I greeted him by name and waved my hand in front of his face to see whether his eyes would track my hand. Perhaps a bit. Then, one at a time, I held herbs under his nose, careful not to touch his nose, as his mother had indicated that we shouldn't do that. Each of the herbs elicited a strong reaction, with Khalid closing his eyes and holding them closed momentarily after each sniffing each plant. The sage may have provoked the most pronounced response.

A few days later, we met in the hall. Khalid was again in his wheelchair, having just come from physical therapy. His mother greeted me eagerly. Before I began working with Khalid, his mother showed me on her phone a photo of Khalid with

his wife and children. His mother and another man (perhaps his father) were also in the picture. Khalid looked healthy and handsome, sporting a closely cropped beard and a colorful athletic jacket. His wife was a beautiful young woman with an artfully draped pink hijab. "He's so handsome," I said to his mother. And, shaking my head, added, "This is so sad. It must be so hard for you." With teary eyes, she nodded her head and touched her hand to her heart.

As had become our custom, I held individual herbs under Khalid's nose. This time, his response to the scent was indisputable—he closed his eyes and held them shut for a moment after each sprig. His mother now asked me to gently touch his nose with the leaves. Like the first time, this provoked a dramatic reaction. He jerked his head back and made a loud breathing noise. In addition to leaves, I brought with me a bright red pentas flower to try to test his ability to follow an object with his eyes, and thus stimulate his vision. I held the flower about 8 inches from his face and slowly moved it from right to left in front of him. There was no question that Khalid's eyes followed the brilliant blossoms. His mother and I glanced at one another. With tears in her eyes, she faced heavenward, touched her hands to her lips and her heart, and mouthed a prayer.

Several months passed. Twice a week, I met with Khalid and his mother. I gave him herbs to smell and showed him brightly colored flowers. Unfortunately, Khalid's condition had not improved. Each time I greeted his mother, her eyes evinced increased despair. The spark of hope diminished even as she lovingly called his name and said the name of the herb I held under his nose.

When I arrived at the unit one day, the occupational therapist called me aside to tell me that Khalid had unexpectedly died a few days earlier. It was a blow. I had so wished, against the odds, that he would recover brain function and eventually go home to his family. I felt for his mother, who sat at his side every day and talked to him, who hoped against hope to win back her active, handsome son. And I thought about his young widow in the stylish pink hijab and his beautiful wide-eyed children who barely knew their father.

I sent his mother my condolences on WhatsApp and concluded, "*Al-bakiya fi hiyatik* [I am sorry for your loss.]"

His mother replied, "Thank you dear Anne for your prayers and kind support. May Allah SWT grant him peace and heaven. *Shakar Allah saeyjusaeykum, Allah yarhamuh wayuhasin alih.* [Thank God will reward you, may God have mercy on him and bless him.]"

Chapter 15

Yulia and Getis

The occupational therapist on the complex medical unit suggested one day that I work with Yulia, in room 5. The room contained three beds, one along each wall. In the bed opposite the entrance lay a patient who was seemingly asleep. A Russian drama was playing on the television above her bed. I approached and whispered, "Yulia?" The figure in the bed opened her eyes slightly and looked vaguely in my direction. "Good morning, Yulia. My name is Anne." She looked at me, bewildered. She seemed drugged. I wasn't sure whether my presence even registered with her.

Yulia appeared to be in her 40s. Short, straight brown hair framed her smooth pale face. I noticed that she had a feeding tube in her nose and a trach tube in her throat. Her hands were enclosed in soft cloth mitts. I held up a rose so that she could see it. She reached out with her mitted hand, trying with a jerky, uncontrolled gesture to grasp the flower. I carefully opened the Velcro strap that secured the mitt and slid her hand out of its restraint. With a swift motion that took me by surprise, Yulia grabbed the flower from my hand with her long, elegant alabaster fingers and brought it to her nose. "I don't think this flower has any fragrance," I told her apologetically. I'm not sure she understood, as I was speaking in Hebrew, and she apparently only speaks Russian. It didn't seem to matter. Yulia was preoccupied with caressing the flower, touching its petals and clutching its stem.

I pushed the button to raise the head of the bed, so that she would be a bit more upright. Then I took the rose back and showed her a violet. She did the same thing, whisking the purple flower out of my hand, bringing it to her nose, and aggressively holding the petals, as if desperate for any sensation. After retrieving the violet, I gently replaced her hand in the mitt. "I'll make you a bouquet you can put next to your bed," I told her. I placed a piece of floral sponge in a small plastic cup, and one at a time, took flowers from my cart, showed them to her, and inserted them in the sponge. I held the miniature arrangement up for her to see. She smiled timidly. I placed the cup on the windowsill next to her bed. "I'll see you next week, Yulia." Her eyes followed me out of the room.

Though she looked younger, Yulia was 54 years old. She had been a champion figure skater in Russia, but an injury ended her career. She then became a skating coach. Shortly after they immigrated to Israel, Yulia's husband was struck by a car, leaving her a widow with two children. She became an alcoholic and drug addict. Her children searched for food in trash cans. Eventually, she overcame her addictions and found work as a house cleaner. She was living with a partner and had resumed

contact with her son when she suffered a ruptured aneurism that resulted in her hospitalization at the rehab center.

The next time I visited Yulia, I brought herbs as well as flowers. Again, each time I showed her a small bunch of basil or mint, she would reach out assertively, grab the cutting from my hand, and hold it under her nose. She inhaled deeply. Then, as was our custom, I would arrange a small bouquet for her and leave it on the sill where she could see it from her bed. There were days when Yulia was very agitated and didn't want me to give her flowers. At other times, it seemed she couldn't get enough of them and would cast a sad look in my direction as I wheeled the cart out of the room.

More than most patients, Yulia seemed despondent. Her face retained its classic beauty, but her almond-shaped brown eyes betrayed her suffering. She often appeared to be in a hazy world of her own. She could speak, but the restraints on her hands limited her ability to gesture. Although the TV above her bed was always on, I never saw her looking at it. Yulia's melancholy isolation left me feeling powerless, wishing there was more I could do for her.

Like Yulia, Getis was confined to his bed. He, too, shared a room with two other patients, both of whom slept all the time. I approached his bed and saw a youthful-looking man lying flat on his back. He had black hair and several days' growth of black beard. Large, thick, black-rimmed glasses framed his wide-open dark eyes, which were staring up at the ceiling. "Getis," I said. He turned and looked in my direction with a hint of a smile on his face. I introduced myself. He looked at the flowers I had in my hand and smiled more broadly. Would you like me to make you a bouquet? He nodded, silently mouthing, "Yes."

Getis is 54 years old, a divorced father of several teenage children. A needy innocence in his expression gave him the look of someone much younger. I was told he had a history of alcohol and drug abuse. Prior to that, he was employed by the army, working in the kitchen. Getis was hospitalized following a train accident and a stroke. He is fully cognitively aware but unable to speak. He makes unintelligible sounds and mouths words. The staff on the unit told me that he loves music, flowers, and fragrances. They added that he is eager to be released. Sadly, years have passed since I was told that, and he is still in his bed, staring at the ceiling.

As with Yulia, I would show Getis each flower before inserting it into the sponge in the cup. He would smile appreciatively and mouth a word or two about how beautiful it was. When the bouquet was complete, I asked if he would like me to put it on the stand next to his bed. "Yes," he mouthed, and "thank you."

Getis also enjoyed smelling herbs. One at a time, I would hold various fragrant herbs under his nose. He inhaled deeply, smiled, and closed his eyes momentarily. Again, after smelling the herbs, he silently thanked me.

I leave Getis's room touched by the sincerity of his voiceless "thank you" and with a sense of impotence. Then I put myself in his place and think of how enormously isolated he must be and how truly powerless he is. He can barely communicate and is unable to do anything for himself, let alone for anyone else.

Chapter 16

Gardening Therapy Is Not for Everyone

One day I learned about a new patient in the complex medical unit who used to own a flower shop. The therapist in the unit thought Hagar would be the perfect candidate for gardening therapy. With great anticipation, I wheeled my cart into Hagar's room. I saw a woman, her head mostly bald (from chemo or radiation therapy, I surmised), sitting with her legs dangling over the side of the bed. Her leathery, tan face was deeply lined, giving her a tough appearance. I guessed her to be in her mid-70s, but the records gave her age as 83. From the look of her pajama top, it appeared that she had had a mastectomy. An IV dripped fluids into her left hand.

"Good morning, Hagar," I greeted her. "My name is Anne. I am a gardening therapist." She glowered at me. "I was wondering if you'd like to make a bouquet." She surveyed the pickle jars of cut flowers on my cart and clearly was not impressed. "I understand you owned a flower shop?" I ventured tentatively.

"Yeah," she replied gruffly, barely raising her head to acknowledge my presence.

"I'm sure you're used to working with a much more varied array of flowers..." She motioned to the flowers.

"Okay, give it to me..." I handed her a small cup and a floral arranging sponge, which she pushed into the bottom of the cup. She took one of the jars of flowers from the top of the cart and turned it in her hand, her long, artificial nails clicking on the glass. With a look of resignation, she pulled one flower, then another, then another, and then some fern fronds from the jar, her hands flying in well-rehearsed motions. In an instant, Hagar had fashioned a glorious, artfully arranged bouquet in that small plastic cup, worthy of being a centerpiece at a wedding.

"Wow!" I exclaimed. "You've created something from nothing!"

"I used to do this all the time," she replied nonchalantly, unmoved.

"Hagar, did you know there is a garden on the roof? Perhaps you'd like to meet with me there next week?"

"I hope I won't still be in the hospital next week. I'm just here for IV antibiotics," she replied hoarsely.

"I hope you'll be discharged by then, too. But, if you're still here, maybe we'll meet in the garden."

"Fine," she grunted.

The following week, a volunteer wheeled Hagar up to the garden. A scarf loosely covered her bald head to protect it from the sun. We toured the garden. She looked around, turned to me, and said, "Are you mocking me?" I was taken aback. "We had REAL flowers—roses and lilies—in our shop. We made bouquets for weddings and all kinds of high-class events," she boasted.

Hagar had a point. While our garden is lush and green, and a delightful contrast to the drab interior of the rehab facility, in the early fall it looked less colorful than it does in other seasons. There simply were not many flowers in bloom. The few roses we had were wilting and sad. And there were no lilies of any kind.

I wheeled Hagar to the herb corner, where we cut sprigs of various herbs that she could plant. We took the cuttings to the table I'd set up with pots, soil, a spade, and a watering can. Hagar refused the apron I offered her and did not want gloves. With her bare hands and long nails, she scooped soil into the small pots. "I like to get my hands dirty," she explained. I told her I did, too. (Another patient, an upbeat white-haired lady in the geriatric rehab unit, once said to me that gardening wearing gloves is like making love with a condom!) Hagar filled several pots with soil and planted an assortment of herbs in each pot. I tagged them with her name and told her I would put them in the greenhouse. Hagar used the remaining time of our session to arrange another stunning bouquet from the assorted small flowers I had cut. "That's magnificent!" I gushed.

"It's nothing," she frowned.

Since Hagar was my last patient of the morning, I wheeled her back down to the unit. She held her bouquet on her lap. I told her I hoped we'd meet again next week in the garden. "I hope to be discharged before next week," was her response. When we got to her room, she set the flower arrangement on her bedstand, picked up her cigarettes, and wheeled herself to the elevator to go out to the smoking area.

The next week, I asked the occupational therapist to arrange for Hagar to come up to the garden for her session. In response, I received a message that Hagar wasn't interested. Later, I saw her sitting in her wheelchair in the courtyard, smoking. I said hello. She ignored me. I felt a bit hurt and dejected. Clearly, neither the garden nor I had made an impression on her. This incident brought home to me another of my personality traits. I'm a people pleaser. And, when I don't succeed in pleasing someone,

147

I feel I've failed.

A few months later, Hagar sat with a scowl on her face in her wheelchair in the common room. Next to her was a patient enthusiastically arranging bouquets. She watched as the other woman selected blossoms from the jars of cut flowers I'd set on the table. To my surprise, Hagar asked for a container and sponge so she, too, could arrange flowers. Unlike her neighbor, who seemed transported by the beauty of the flowers and who took pains to carefully select flowers that complemented one another in color and shape, Hagar seemed not to pay attention to the flowers themselves. She worked deftly and created harmonious combinations of flowers from her years of experience as a florist, but I did not sense that she enjoyed what she was doing. It was merely a practiced way to keep her hands busy. Though I praised her creations profusely, as they were truly lovely and original, she did not evince any pleasure or satisfaction. Gardening therapy, I said to myelf, is not for everyone. And it's often difficult to predict who will respond to this therapeutic modality.

The following week, a hint of a smile crossed Hagar's lips when I pushed my cart full of flowers and plants into the common room. She asked for materials and energetically began making beautiful arrangements. She also took the remains of the previous weeks' bouquets from the windowsill and salvaged what she could to complement the fresh flowers. For the first time, she interacted with other patients at the table. She watched the woman across from her pulling a seedling out of a small pot. "Don't pull it that way. You'll tear the roots," she cautioned her. "You should squeeze the pot to get the plant out," she said, demonstrating with her fingers.

Hagar's engagement in the gardening activity was a big step for her. But her relationship with other patients represented even greater progress. The other therapists on the unit were delighted and amazed. Until then, most of what one heard from Hagar were complaints—about boredom, about not wanting to be in the hospital. This time, glancing at the trays of freshly rooted cuttings, she said, "This is what I really love—working with plants." After completing five or six attractive arrangements in the yogurt cups I supplied, Hagar said she was tired. "You've accomplished a lot," I observed.

"No, I didn't accomplish a lot. This is nothing," she reflected. "Back in the day, for the holidays, I used to make arrangements from here to there," she said proudly, with an expansive sweep of her hand.

Chapter 17

An Outpatient Therapy Group

Unfortunately, another wave of COVID had struck. Most of the inpatient units in the hospital were quarantined, the patients stuck inside without visitors or therapists. Outpatient activities continued for those willing to come to the hospital and subject to a negative antigen test at the entrance. In addition, the weather was unusually cold, with steady, heavy rain. Three stalwart patients out of the usual seven or eight showed up on this day for their outpatient gardening group therapy session. Ze'ev, a portly, pink-faced man with white hair who walked with a limp, was seated at the table when I entered the room. Dahlia, a wrinkled but distinguished-looking lady in her early 70s with dark, slightly graying hair, arrived, an attendant pushing her in her wheelchair. And finally, Dudu (a common Israeli nickname for David), a man in his late 40s, his weary face accented by a short salt-and-pepper beard, a large knit yarmulka on his head, struggled into the room, supported by a pair of crutches. He wore a gray zip-up hoodie with English lettering and blue workman's pants.

This was my first meeting with this group, as I was substituting for their usual therapist who was in quarantine. After introductions, I told the group that in honor of *Tu B'Shvat* we would be making small flower arrangements to be distributed to patients on the units in quarantine. The Jewish holiday of Tu B'Shvat, the fifteenth day of the Hebrew month of Shvat[5], is known as the "new year for trees," usually falls during January.

What is the new year for trees? In the nineteenth century, with the beginning of the Zionist movement, as more Jews returned to their ancient homeland, the holiday became a time to plant trees. Jews living outside Israel often collected money to be donated to the Jewish National Fund to support the planting of trees and reforestation in Israel. It was also an occasion to enjoy the fruits characteristic of the land of Israel: grapes, figs, pomegranates, olives, and dates. Some have adopted the custom of having a special meal on Tu B'Shvat at which those fruits are featured. In more recent times, Tu B'Shvat has become the Israeli Arbor Day, or even a local version of Earth Day. Students, beginning in preschool, plant trees and other plants and proudly watch them grow and develop. At a shopping mall in Tel Aviv, groups of schoolchildren come throughout the day to plant small saplings in large buckets, which are brought to the mall's roof garden. For gardening therapists, Tu B'Shvat is our holiday. On this day, everyone gets into the gardening spirit.

Each of the three expressed enthusiasm for the project. "We're doing a real *mitzvah* (good deed)," Dudu said. "It's wonderful that we can help other people." Simply making flower arrangements can be a useful therapeutic activity. It involves small motor skills, thought, planning, aesthetic sensibility, and creativity. The product is visually pleasing and, when herbs are part of the mix, fragrant, too. However, when the activity has a purpose beyond the product itself—to make a beautiful gift for patients in isolation—the exercise becomes meaningful. According to Viktor Frankl (*Man's Search for Meaning*), it is meaning that has the greatest therapeutic effect, even on a small scale like this.

---

5   The significance of the date derives from Jewish law related to the timing of the required tithes given from produce. The fruits that ripened from Tu B'Shvat on were counted for the following year's tithes.

In the center of the large table around which the three were seated were trays full of flowers, herbs, and colorful foliage I'd collected in the garden. I cut flimsy disposable plastic drinking cups to form small shallow containers, which sat in piles on the table. There was also a box full of small cubes of green floral foam, used for flower arranging. I put a cube of foam into a cup and added water to soak the foam. I selected a bright pink and red pentas floret and jammed its stem into the foam. Then I added a fragrant, light-green lemon geranium leaf, a branch of basil, and a sprig of lavender. Voilà, a bouquet. This served as a model, but I encouraged the patients to be as creative as they wanted with the materials on the table.

They applied themselves energetically to the task of making the bouquets. Dahlia, despite having the use of only one hand, worked deftly. As she selected flowers or foliage to include in her arrangements, she spoke to them, "Come here, little hunchback, we'll straighten you out," she said, manipulating the scissors with her one functional hand to cut the curled stem on a sweet potato leaf so it would stand erect in the foam.

"Oh, you lovely flower, you will look so nice next to this leaf." "Here, stand next to your friend." When she selected a cutting of the vine colloquially called "Wandering Jew," Dahlia addressed it, "Hello, little wanderer. We've found a home for you," as she tucked it into the green foam in the cup. When she discovered a large snail among the leaves and stems, we put it in a container, from which it tried to escape. Dahlia said to the snail, "You enemy, you. Don't try to get out and do mischief."

Meanwhile, Dudu was arranging charming little bouquets at a furious rate. In response to my questions, he told me a bit about himself. He had been a delivery truck driver before the accident that caused his injury two years ago. Since then, he has been unable to work. But, he said, "I don't just sit around the house, God forbid. Despite my pain, I need to be active." He continued, "I study Talmud and other Jewish texts. I help around the house." Dudu told me that he has "six children, thank God, ages 3 to 21."

The group discussion turned to Tu B'Shvat. Dudu commented that the holiday makes him happy. It's a time of new beginnings and growth. We look forward to that moment when the fruit the trees will bear. "Plants fill us with hope," he said. Surveying the dozen colorful bouquets he had made, Dudu again said, "It's so satisfying to be able to do something for someone else." Finally, he noted that this would be his last day in the group. He had finished his course of outpatient therapy at the hospital. He had been coming for a long time and received care in many units. "I can't tell you how much I appreciate the wonderful care I received here. Everyone was so good to me. You have all helped me so much."

We made tea from herbs picked in the garden and drank a toast to Dudu's recovery and good health and to his family. "May they all be healthy, happy, and successful."

The following week, I was again working with the outpatient group. About fifteen minutes before the session was scheduled to begin, Mordechai, a man in his early 60s with a dark complexion and salt and pepper hair topped by a knit *kippah*, was wheeled into the room by a tall Indian attendant. I noticed that Mordechai's right arm hung limp at his side (he was recovering from a stroke.) Since we had some time before the others arrived, I introduced myself and chatted a bit with him. Orit, the gardening therapist who regularly works with groups, brought Mordechai a dried leaf from a plant in the garden. Mordechai immediately recognized it as "qat" or "khat." Orit explained that for some reason, the plant had failed to thrive in the hospital's roof garden.

I had no idea what "qat" was, but Mordechai was happy to enlighten me. "Yemenite people chew it," he explained with a smile. Only the young, tender leaves are chewed. "It relaxes you," he continued. "Like when the kids are out of control, it doesn't matter." However, he added, "If you chew it before bed, you won't be able to sleep." I asked Mordechai if he was from Yemen. "No, I was born in Israel," he replied, "but my parents came here from Yemen." In most countries, qat is an illegal drug, like hashish. At one time, Israel attempted to outlaw qat, but there was tremendous pushback as it is such a fundamental part of Yemenite culture. "In Yemenite society, if you don't chew qat, you're not part of social events." When he was younger, Mordechai's family had 5 dunams (1.25 acres) of qat under cultivation in the Carmel region of Israel. Some of his friends tried to sell qat in Europe, but they were arrested. A small bunch, he said, sells for 50 shekels ($15).

As the time for the group to begin approached, the other participants drifted into the room. A tall, slim, handsome young man with dark hair and glasses, wearing a Puma sweatsuit, walked in slowly, leaning heavily on his two crutches. He introduced himself to us, saying his name was Yosef and that this was his first time attending a gardening therapy group. We welcomed him warmly.

Gil, an attractive woman in her 20s with luxuriant black hair gathered in a loose bun on the top of her head, entered next, aided by a pair of walking sticks. Her beautiful dark eyes and eyebrows were visible above her COVID mask. Ze'ev and Dahlia, who had participated in the group the previous week, were also there. This time, I noticed that Ze'ev was favoring one arm. Ya'akov entered the room in his motorized wheelchair, accompanied by his wife, who pulled up a chair and joined the group at the table. Ya'akov, like Dahlia, could use only one arm. Finally, Yaeli, a short and slightly plump twenty-something, well-groomed and nicely made-up woman joined the group. She was recovering from injuries sustained in a car accident.

Since Yosef was new to the group, he was asked to introduce himself. "My name is Yosef, but my friends call me 'Yossi.' I'm 30 years old. I'm here being treated for chronic pain." When asked if he had any gardening experience, he replied, "My girlfriend and I used to have plants in our garden, but we now live in an apartment building, so we only have indoor plants." The others around the table introduced themselves by name.

Pointing to the table covered with small pots of tiny vegetables, Orit explained that today the group would be working with "winter vegetables"—celery, broccoli, sorrel, bok choy, lettuce, spinach, radishes, green onions, carrots, and kale. There was a discussion about some of the differences between "winter vegetables" and "summer vegetables." Of the former, we eat the leaves, stems, and roots or tubers, and sometimes the flowers, as with broccoli and cauliflower. The edible parts of summer vegetables are usually the fruit, that is, the seed-bearing part of the plant. On the table were also containers of radish, carrot, and spinach seeds. Orit pointed out that one must use caution planting spinach seeds as they have sharp thorns. There ensued a discussion of how a sharp, prickly seed could yield a lush, green, tender, and tasty plant. There were also bunches of celery, whose base could be cut off and planted. Those who did not want to plant seeds or transplant the small plants into larger pots mixed potting soil with humus—organic fertilizer—for the others to use.

I was impressed by how quickly everyone got to work. And more impressive was the way in which the members of the group cooperated with one another. Dahlia, working with one hand, filled pots with soil for Ya'akov and Mordechai to use for planting. They watered one another's plants and seeds. Ze'ev mixed the potting soil for everyone's use. Orit encouraged him to use his weak arm. Although standing was generally difficult for Yossi and Gil, they both stood while they worked as it was easier for them to reach the plants and supplies. And no one complained. In fact, everyone was so absorbed in their tasks and in lively conversation that they seemed to have forgotten about their pain and limitations, at least until they had to pick up their crutches or walking sticks to leave. Several people elected to take their freshly planted seeds or transplanted vegetables home with them.

A couple of months later, when I entered the elevator with my cart full of flowers, I saw Yossi from the group standing with his crutch. I greeted him and asked how he was doing. "Doing well," he immediately replied with a sparkle in his eye. He admired the flowers on the cart and said, "My girlfriend and I are getting married next month."

"Mazal tov! (congratulations)," I responded.

"Look at our wedding invitation." He took out his phone and showed me an image of the invitation, which had delicate pink flowers interwoven with the text. I asked if he had designed the beautiful invitation. He told me a friend had made the illustrations for them. "Flowers mean so much to us," he told me, glancing again at the assortment on my cart.

Chapter 18

Bringing Out the Inner Farmer

The therapy group on the geriatric rehabilitation unit has a different dynamic from that of the outpatient therapy or complex medical unit groups. These are older patients who are hospitalized
for relatively brief periods—weeks or months—for rehabilitation
from injuries or surgery. As a result of the shorter hospitalizations,
the composition of the group is quite fluid, changing almost
weekly. The patients tend to be optimistic. They see the progress
they have made and look forward to being discharged from the
institution. While they are elderly, and in some cases very old,
they are generally cognitively intact and healthy aside from the
specific injury for which they are being treated. The goals of my
work with this group are threefold: 1) occupational—using their
hands, arms, and small muscles; 2) social—fostering interaction
among the patients; and 3) psychological—providing an opportunity for creativity and a sense of competence.

Between three and six patients participate in the group each week. They wheel themselves (or are wheeled) or walk with a walker to a table in the common room of the unit. I ask those assembled to introduce themselves and describe their current mood in a single word. "Good," "Not bad," "Alright" were the responses I received on one recent occasion. I then explain the activity for the day. I try to center each week's session around a theme, with a choice of tasks related to the theme. Thus, one day was devoted to the herbs za'atar and thyme. Another session focused on geraniums. A few weeks later, we talked about and planted basil.

The activities combine working with the plants and flowers or seeds—planting, making cuttings—with conversation. This tends to be a talkative group, and I often need to moderate the discussion to be sure everyone has an opportunity to speak. A distinguished-looking white-haired gentleman, sitting erect in his wheelchair in a crisply ironed plaid sports shirt, introduced himself as Eliezer. Surveying the pots, plants, soil, and spades I'd arranged on the table, he issued a disclaimer. "I'm not a farmer," he said. Nevertheless, he plunged enthusiastically into the tasks of filling the small pots with soil, cutting sprigs of za'atar and thyme, planting them meticulously and watering them with care. As he worked, he spoke in a clear, modulated voice, in refined, if slightly accented Hebrew. "This reminds me of planting herbs in the garden with my mother as a young boy in Czechoslovakia before the war. But we didn't have za'atar or thyme."

Eliezer is 93, though from his appearance and demeanor, one would guess he is at least ten years younger. "We lived in a small village," he continues. "I helped my mother plant herbs in the yard outside our house."

"Aha, you *were* a farmer!" I respond. The group begins speculating about what herbs and vegetables Eliezer's mother might have been growing in her kitchen garden in Czechoslovakia in the 1930s.

Eliezer then recounted the story of how his family fled Czechoslovakia for Hungary when the Germans invaded.

(He speaks both Czech and Hungarian, as well as several other languages.) The others in the group, which included a woman from Morocco and a couple of native-born Israelis, reacted to his story. "From Hungary, we were deported to Auschwitz," he explained calmly. "Fortunately, the war was almost over, and we were liberated before long. After liberation, we found ourselves in the Soviet Union."

"Wow! That's quite a story. When did you come to Israel?" I asked.

"In 1972."

This group session took place a few days before *Yom HaShoah*, Israel's national Holocaust Memorial Day. Eliezer announced proudly that he was going to be interviewed on national television that day—"Channel 11 at 11:30 am," he told me. I explained that, unfortunately, I was going to be on a hike that day. "No problem," he said, "you can record it!"

The discussion turned back to herbs. Nomi, the woman from Morocco, who introduced herself as an expert in gardening, gave the group some lessons in planting and cooking with herbs. With great excitement, she pointed to a tomato seedling that had spouted in the large pot of za'atar, from which they were taking cuttings. I told her that she could repot the tomato plant. With experienced hands, she removed the tiny plant and repotted it. I put a tag in the pot with her name and the date so that she could follow its progress.

At the end of the session, the members of the group surveyed the rows of small pots, each with a tiny sprig of za'atar or thyme. I tagged the pots with the patients' names and asked them again to describe their mood in a single word.

"Excellent!" declared one woman.

"Uplifted," said Eliezer.

And Arik, who at the beginning was skeptical about his ability to do gardening with one weak hand, said he felt "reborn!"

The next time we met, I noticed Eliezer approaching the table, walking confidently with a walker. "Wow, you've come

a long way," I said. "Last week you were in a wheelchair."

"Yes," he smiled proudly, "and I'm going to be discharged in two weeks!"

"That's wonderful!" "Not only are you making good progress," I announced, "but the cuttings you planted a few weeks ago have made progress, too. They have all grown roots and are ready to be repotted."

I had brought the small pots with thyme and za'atar Eliezer had planted a month earlier. I gave him pots, potting soil, and a spade, and he set to work, gently removing the young plants, and planting them ever so carefully in the larger pots. As he lovingly watered each plant, I talked to him about his career. He had been a violin teacher at music conservatories in Russia and later in various cities in Israel. His wife taught piano. They also played together in a trio.

"Do you still play the violin?" I inquired.

"No," he shook his head, "you really need to practice every day, and I haven't been able to practice for some time."

I told Eliezer he could bring his plants home with him. He looked at the bright green za'atar plants standing upright in their pots and thought about it. "I could take one home, but what would I do with it?" he reflected. "The only herb we use at home is parsley!" I suggested that it's good in pasta. He considered it further and decided to take home one pot.

When I came to the unit for the next week's group meeting, I saw Eliezer talking animatedly with other patients. "Eliezer, you're still here!" I said.

"I'm leaving in a few hours."

"Congratulations! Much good health!" I asked if he would like to join the group one last time, but he was too excited about his impending departure to focus on gardening.

The day of Eliezer's discharge, the other two members of the group were also in particularly good moods. Shoshana told me that she was going to be discharged in two days, and Arik said he would be going home in six days. This was the last gardening session for both. The previous week, Arik, who said he felt "reborn" after one of our sessions, sat in his wheelchair in the courtyard and declined to join the gardening therapy group. This week, however, as I pushed my cart past him in the courtyard, I showed him trays of bright green basil that he had planted as cuttings a few weeks earlier. His face brightened. "Yes, I'll join the group," he assured me.

At the appointed hour, he was already seated at the table in his wheelchair. With a grin, he surveyed the trays of seedlings bearing tags with his name. I demonstrated how to remove the small plants from the tiny pots and transplant them into larger pots. He was impressed by the tight ball of roots that had grown from the cuttings, which had no roots at all when he planted it just a few weeks earlier. He also noted that some of the leaves had holes in them. Clearly, someone in the garden found these tender leaves to be tasty—an insect, or more likely, a snail. With a small pair of pruning shears, Arik delicately held each imperfect leaf and snipped it off.

I encouraged him to use his weaker left hand (he had broken his shoulder when he injured his leg) to hold the leaf while he manipulated the shears in his right. Soon, he was routinely using his left hand to assist in planting and watering. He commented that this represented a big step for him, as he still may require surgery on that shoulder.

As he filled the pots with soil, planted, and watered, Arik recalled that when he was young, his father's brother let him help tend the plants in his garden. He also told me that he was an only child and that on his mother's birthday and for shabbat, he would bring home huge bouquets of flowers for her. She loved the flowers. "You know," he confided, "flowers really make people feel good."

By the end of the session, Arik had repotted nine basil plants. I told him he was welcome to take them home. He was delighted and said he would take all of them. He asked me how to care for these plants at home—how frequently to water them, what kind of light they need, etc. I also instructed him on cutting them back regularly to keep them thick and bushy. I wished Arik and Shoshana (who was also taking her six plants home with her) good luck and good health. Arik responded, "I enjoyed this so much! It was thrilling to see the progress of the plants I planted myself." "I might come back to the rehab every Tuesday just to do gardening," he added with a wink.

Chapter 19

A Sweet New Year

Some of the patients in the geriatric rehab unit noticed on my cart
a collage, which my patient Ahuva had made using all kinds of
interesting plant materials. They wanted to do something similar.
The following week, I brought containers of seeds, pods, dried
leaves, bark, twigs, dried flowers, beans, and the like, which I put
in the center of the table. I gave each patient a piece of cardboard
and a bottle of glue and explained that we would be making
collages. I encouraged them to be as creative as they wished,
making pictures, abstract designs or whatever came to mind. I
was struck by the beauty and originality of their creations. Some
filled the board with a mixture of densely packed materials, and
others fashioned minimalistic designs.

Ron, a new patient on the unit, sat upright in his wheelchair, a stiff plastic collar supporting his neck. He worked slowly and quietly, not saying a word. In fact, I wasn't sure he was able to speak. I noticed that he had squeezed dots of glue on the board in front of him and used the point of his scissors to meticulously spread the glue into very precise shapes. He then gingerly sprinkled rice, lentils and other small seeds on the glue. He shook off the excess seeds, and I could see that he had carefully "written" with glue and seeds the word "MIRIAM," his wife's name.

"Wow!" I exclaimed, genuinely impressed with what he'd done. He smiled proudly and continued writing letters with the glue. This time, instead of seeds, he cut tiny pieces of the dried stems of garlic flowers, and used them to form the words, "FROM ME". As I began to lavish praise on him for his clever and original use of the materials, he replied to me softly. He told me that he's a man of letters, not an artist. He writes poetry and had written children's books for his grandchildren. I learned later that Ron was in rehab following an accident in which he had broken his neck. Among other damage, the injury had limited his ability to use his hands. The occupational therapist on the unit was thrilled to see him using the fine muscles in his fingers to do the delicate work of fashioning this card for his wife.

After the success of the collage activity, I decided to do a similar activity with the geriatric rehab group on another unit. This time, when I introduced the activity, I mentioned that a patient on the other unit had used the materials to form words. Since it was just before the Jewish New Year, the patients all chose to make New Year's greeting cards with the materials I had provided. The range of results was impressive, but everyone included in their collage some variation of "Happy New Year!" The patients kept their creations to share with loved ones or staff on the unit.

The pomegranate (in Hebrew, *rimon*), in addition to being a beautiful fruit, is strongly associated with the Jewish

New Year. (*Rimon* is also the Hebrew word for a hand grenade.) It grows abundantly in Israel and ripens around the time of the New Year, in late August and September. Over the generations, the pomegranate has taken on many symbolic meanings. Because it contains many seeds, it is often seen as a symbol of fertility and abundance. There is a legend that a pomegranate contains 613 seeds, corresponding to the 613 commandments in the Torah. It is therefore, to some, a symbol of knowledge, righteousness, and wisdom. Many people include a pomegranate as one of the foods eaten at dinner on the first night of Rosh Hashanah (the Jewish New Year), as an omen that we should have as many virtues as the number of seeds in the pomegranate so that we will merit being blessed with a good year.

Because of its seasonal resonance, I generally plan an activity involving pomegranates around the time of the New Year. While a bit messy because of all the red juice they contain, it is easy to plant pomegranate seeds. After discussing the symbolic meaning of the fruit and its connection to the holiday, I show the patients how to cut off the top. Once the top is off, one can see that the pomegranate has sections, like a citrus fruit. If you cut along the pulp that divides the sections, they can be easily pulled apart and the seeds extracted. In fact, the small, juicy bits that comprise the pomegranate are not the seeds. They are the fruit. Each tiny red fruit contains a white seed. In order for the seed to germinate, the red fruit and juice must be completely removed from the seed. I demonstrate to the patients how to remove the fruit and juice by rolling each little fruit between their fingers or in a paper towel. Once the white seed has been removed, it can be planted directly in soil in a small pot. The soil must be kept moist. After the patients plant their seeds, I put the pots in the greenhouse. The seeds usually sprout within a couple of weeks.

A few weeks after he made his collage for his wife, Ron was one of the patients in the group planting pomegranate seeds. He applied himself to the task with enthusiasm, working delicately and meticulously to remove all the fruit, so that the seeds were perfectly clean and white. I could see the improvement in his fine motor skills. While still working slowly, his fingers moved with more confidence. He carefully planted only two seeds in each small pot, as per my instructions. (Many patients have trouble with that and tend to dump a pile of seeds in each small pot. If all the seeds sprout, the roots will not have room to develop.) Several of the patients tired after filling one or two trays of seedling pots. Ron, however, was eager to continue until the time for the session had ended. He told me how much he enjoyed the activity. I wheeled him back to his room, where he insisted that I take a piece of the honey cake, a traditional Jewish New Year treat, from the container on his bedside table. "It's not from a store, you know. My wife made it." And, indeed, it was delicious.

170

Chapter 20

Give me work!

An obese, gruff-looking woman with a dark complexion and a gray crocheted beret covering much of her equally gray hair, sat wedged into an extra-wide wheelchair at a table in the common room of the complex medical unit. Her large fleshy hands dexterously placed small mosaic tiles on a piece of plywood. Pushing my cart of flowers, plants, and soil, I approached her: "Ella?"

"Yes," she said raising her head from her project. "Would you like to arrange flowers?"

"I would," she replied in Hebrew, heavily inflected with a Russian accent. She smiled, and her dark eyes glowed as she surveyed the colorful flowers in the jars on my cart.

I handed Ella several small cups and green floral arranging sponges. She carefully placed a sponge in each cup, to which I added water. Then, deliberately but quickly, she selected flowers, one at a time, trimmed the stems as necessary, and placed them in the cups. Ella's aesthetic sense was readily apparent in her careful grouping of flowers of complementary colors and shapes. The result was a collection of stunning small bouquets. Ella admired them with pride and pleasure. I asked if she would like to plant. She enthusiastically said she would. I told her that next time I'd bring cuttings for her to plant. "Wonderful!" she said.

As soon as Ella sees me pushing my cart of supplies into the unit, she looks me in the eye and beckons me with her large hands: "Give me work!" And work she does, as quickly as I can supply her with materials. Ella deftly and efficiently planted herb and coleus cuttings, transplanted small broccoli plants into larger pots, and continued to arrange artful bouquets in small applesauce containers. She asked me to place the bouquets on the windowsill in the common room, where everyone could enjoy her handiwork.

Ella needs to keep her hands busy. One day when I

arrived in the unit, she was seated at the table meticulously tearing, folding, and stacking roll after roll of paper towels. She looked up and said she would be ready to start planting as soon as she'd finished the roll she was working on. Evidently, the staff, knowing how important it was to Ella to be "doing something," kept her busy tearing towels for them. She took the job seriously.

She told me that she had come to Israel thirty years ago from Tajikistan. She was employed most of her life as a cook in a restaurant, making traditional Middle Eastern food. When I

asked if she had a family, she replied proudly, "I have a family—six children, twenty-eight grandchildren, and eight great-grandchildren. That's a real family!" I asked her whether she would be spending the upcoming Passover holiday with her family. "Yes!" she enthused. "Home for the holiday."

While Ella applied herself assiduously to the gardening task at hand, she was attentive to the needs of others around her. Seated next to her at the table was a tiny, frail, wizened woman, wearing a knit ski cap and a woolen shawl. I had asked her on occasion whether she was interested in working with plants or flowers. She declined. However, one spring day, my cart was ablaze with geraniums, snapdragons, and a mélange of other brilliantly colored flowers I had picked in the garden atop the rehab center. Ella pointed to the flowers on the cart and, in Russian, asked Tamar—the woman slumped in the wheelchair next to her—whether she wanted to arrange flowers. She agreed immediately.

Although she was busy planting cuttings, as I provided the materials to Tamar, Ella explained to her in Russian how to insert the stems in the sponge and make bouquets.

Tamar's gnarled hands shook as she held the flowers and slowly removed the lower leaves, per Ella's instructions. She succeeded in creating three lovely small arrangements, which then adorned the windowsill in the common room on the unit.

On another occasion, I brought Ella the herb and coleus cuttings she had planted a month earlier. They had grown roots and were ready to be transplanted. I helped Ella put on an apron and watched as she squeezed her enormous hands into a pair of large disposable gloves. She had previously been content to work the soil with her bare hands, but now her massive fingers were adorned with purple nail polish, and she didn't want to spoil her manicure.

I explained the task to her. "Bring what you have!" she commanded me. "When there is no work, there is no life!" she philosophized. Ella worked independently and efficiently. I was always impressed by the delicacy with which she handled small seedings. When she finished repotting a plant and watering it, she would say in her limited Hebrew, "Take it." However, after transplanting the coleus plants, she told me that she wanted to take them home. I suggested she keep them in the unit, but she preferred that I take them back up to garden and bring them back to her once they had grown larger.

A few weeks later, Ella was discharged to the embrace of her large, loving family. She left with her coleus plants in hand.

Epilogue

Often when friends learn that I do gardening therapy, their immediate response is to tell me about the schefflera or dieffenbachia in their living room, whose leaves have suddenly started turning brown. They want me to explain why and advise them on how to treat it. I smile and explain that I don't treat plants. Rather, I provide therapy to people, using plants as the therapeutic modality. "But couldn't you just look at my plant?"

Perhaps I should confess that an aspect of my work—in fact, possibly the most therapeutically efficacious activity I do with patients—does involve treating plants. From time to time, I walk through the roof garden searching for the most pathetic, neglected-looking plants—plants with drooping brown leaves, long, leggy stems, wilted blossoms, often in pots they've outgrown. I collect these unfortunate specimens, load them on my cart together with watering cans, pruning shears, fresh potting soil and pots, and wheel them down to the geriatric rehabilitation unit. When the patients seated around the table on the unit see me approaching with a collection of rather large, if somewhat unsightly plants, they perk up and their eyes sparkle.

I ask if they recognize any of the plants I've set on the table in front of them. Occasionally there is a lingering flower that betrays the identity of the forlorn foliage. Most times, they don't recognize them. I identify the plants and show them photos of what the flowers on each of the plants look like. "These plants are here for treatment and your task today is to rehabilitate them." I explain that they should remove the dead leaves. The leggy branches they cut off can be planted in small pots where they will root. I also point out the plants that need repotting and suggest that most require additional soil and all need to be watered.

The patients dive into the work with intense focus, delicately plucking or cutting off dead leaves one at a time. The ensuing silence around the table is broken only when someone asks me for shears or to pass the watering can. They work meticulously, careful not to miss anything.

Patients who have difficulty using one of their hands suddenly find the strength to hold a branch with one hand and manipulate the shears with the other. I am reminded of the scene in the Wizard of Oz when Dorothy and her companions are in a beauty parlor in the Emerald City, being primped and groomed before their audience with the wizard. As the pruning of a plant approaches completion, the patient who treated it leans back in her wheelchair to admire her handiwork. The plants are transformed, indeed, rehabilitated.

At the end of the session, before I even ask the patients how they feel, they tell me. "I enjoyed this so much," extolled Isaac, a dapper white-haired gentleman, who began the session by telling me his wife was the one who cared for the plants in their garden. "It really lifts the spirit."

"This was such fun," soft-spoken Esther told me, a huge smile on her face.

While the group sessions are scheduled for an hour, most times they end before the hour as patients say they are tired, or that their hands or shoulders hurt. But, when the activity is "plant rehabilitation," everyone is busy for the full hour and still wants more. "Don't you have more plants I can work on?" begged Millie, as I loaded the refreshed plants on my cart.

For several months, I worked individually in the garden with a patient named Shulamit from one of the geriatric rehab units. She loved all facets of gardening, but most of all, she enjoyed revitalizing neglected plants. As she deftly wielded the pruning shears and added soil by the handful, she would talk to me. At first, she shared her frustrations. Formerly a very active and independent 80-year-old, since her fall (on the way to go for a swim), Shulamit has been confined to a wheelchair. She wondered how she'd ever be able to get back home to her second story apartment with its terrace garden. She cried, fearing that she will never be able to live independently again. But as she snipped and trimmed, and made cuttings for planting, she turned to me and said, "You know, when I rehabilitate this plant, I feel I'm rehabilitating myself." Indeed, as the weeks passed, Shulamit gradually began standing for short periods, then walking with a walker, and eventually, walking on her own. She was discharged back to her apartment and her beloved terrace garden.

Addendum

I completed the writing of this book during the months following the horrific Hamas attack on Israel on October 7, 2023. Israel is at war. The beautiful faces of the young soldiers killed the previous day smile out at us from the front page of each day's newspaper. I know that for every one of the soldiers who fell in action, there may be a dozen or more who were injured, many grievously. I have not yet met any of them in my work. But I think about them as I look at the many amputees and head-injured patients in the rehabilitation hospital. Although the names and personal stories behind the numbers do not appear in the newspapers, many of the wounded soldiers will pay a high price all their lives for their courage in defending Israel and protecting its citizens from the terrorists just beyond our borders who seek to annihilate us.

Acknowledgements

I owe my career as a gardening therapist to Einat Golani. Her lecture in 2016 opened my eyes to this field. Einat, coincidentally, supervised my internship and later became my colleague at Reut Rehabilitation Hospital where I work. Orit Eden, another colleague at Reut, has inspired me and has taught me much about dealing with severely compromised patients. Many people have supported and encouraged me in writing this book. I am deeply grateful to Michael Oren who urged me to write the book and offered me invaluable guidance in the writing process. I thank my editor, Ed Levy, and Margherita Buzzi, who designed the cover and the interior layout of the book. My brother, Mike Jacker, prodded and cajoled me throughout my writing and helped me navigate the publication process. He also gave me thoughtful feedback on the manuscript. My sons, Michael and Zvi, read the manuscript and offered helpful comments. My daughter, Ellie, Menachem Wecker, Alfred Tauber and Einat Yehene read portions of the manuscript at early stages of this project and gave me useful advice. Davey Barel and Sara Feller made valuable suggestions about my photographs. Finally, I thank my husband Jonathan for patiently enduring my endless talk about the book, my long evenings upstairs at my desk writing and rewriting and the hours I spent in my studio photographing yet another plant.

About the Author

Anne Dubitzky was born and raised in the Chicago area. She is a graduate of Wellesley College and Harvard Law School. Most of her career was spent as a senior administrator at Massachusetts General Hospital in Boston. In 2009, Anne and her husband moved to Tel Aviv, where she worked briefly in healthcare administration before studying gardening therapy at Seminar HaKibbutzim. She now works on a volunteer basis as a gardening therapist at Reut rehabilitation hospital in Tel Aviv. Anne is also a serious amateur photographer. Additional examples of her photography can be seen at: *annedubitzkyphotography.com*.

www.ingramcontent.com/pod-product-compliance
Lightning Source LLC
Chambersburg PA
CBHW040850120626
46547CB00006B/558